W9-ABV-630

Recent Titles in
Contributions to the Study of World Literature

WRITING AND REALITY

A Study of Modern British Diary Fiction

Andrew Hassam

Contributions to the Study of World Literature,
Number 47

Greenwood Press
Westport, Connecticut • London

Library of Congress Cataloging-in-Publication Data

Hassam, Andrew.
    Writing and reality : a study of modern British diary fiction /
Andrew Hassam.
        p.   cm. — (Contributions to the study of world literature,
    ISSN 0738–9345 ; no. 47)
    Includes bibliographical references (p.   ).
    ISBN 0–313–28540–3 (alk. paper)
    1. English fiction—20th century—History and criticism.   2. Diary
fiction—History and criticism.   3. Diaries in literature.
I. Title.   II. Series.
PR888.D52H37   1993
823'.91409—dc20   92–25764

British Library Cataloguing in Publication Data is available.

Library of Congress Catalog Card Number: 92–25764
ISBN: 0–313–28540–3
ISSN: 0738–9345

First published in 1993

Greenwood Press, 88 Post Road West, Westport, CT 06881
An imprint of Greenwood Publishing Group, Inc.

Printed in the United States of America

The paper used in this book complies with the
Permanent Paper Standard issued by the National
Information Standards Organization (Z39.48–1984).

10 9 8 7 6 5 4 3 2 1

COPYRIGHT ACKNOWLEDGMENTS

The author and publishers are grateful for permission to quote from the following:

The Collector by John Fowles. Copyright © 1963 by John Fowles. Reproduced by permission of Sheil Land Associates Ltd.

"The Diary as Raw Material: Rayner Heppenstall's *The Pier*" by Andrew Hassam. In *Essays in Poetics* 15.2 (1990). Reproduced by permission of the editors.

The Golden Notebook by Doris Lessing. Copyright © 1962 by Doris Lessing. Reproduced by permission of Michael Joseph Ltd. and Simon and Schuster.

The Ice Is Singing by Jane Rogers. Copyright © 1987 by Jane Rogers. Reproduced by permission of Faber and Faber Ltd. and Peters Fraser & Dunlop Ltd.

"Literary Exploration in British Fictive Sea Journals" by Andrew Hassam. In *University of Toronto Quarterly* 19.3 (1988) copyright © 1988, the Board of Governors, The University of Calgary Press. Reproduced by permission of the editor.

Nelly's Version by Eva Figes. Copyright © 1985 by Eva Figes. Reproduced by permission of Hamish Hamilton Ltd. and Rogers, Coleridge & White Ltd.

The Pier by Rayner Heppenstall. Copyright © 1986 by Rayner Heppenstall. Reproduced by permission of Margaret Heppenstall.

Private Papers by Margaret Forster. Copyright © 1986 by Margaret Forster. Reproduced by permission of Chatto & Windus and Margaret Forster.

Three by Ann Quin. Copyright © 1966 by Ann Quin. Reproduced by permission of Marion Boyars Publishers.

The Voyage of the Destiny by Robert Nye. Copyright © 1982 by Robert Nye. Reproduced by permission of Sheil Land Associates Ltd.

Contents

Acknowledgments

This study was written between 1987 and 1989 while I was University of Wales Research Fellow at Saint David's University College, Lampeter, and I am grateful both to the University and to the College for providing me with the necessary research facilities. I am particularly indebted to Kathy Miles in the library for her patience in tracing vital texts and to all the staff of the Department of English at Lampeter for their hospitality and support during a period of general academic pressure. Mr. Gavin Edwards and Professor Robert Sharpe at Lampeter, and Dr. Lyn Pykett at the University College of Wales, Aberystwyth, were kind enough to offer comments on individual draft chapters. A special debt of thanks, however, is due to Mr. Peter Miles, Lecturer in English at Lampeter, for so generously giving of his time and knowledge in overseeing the whole project. Whilst all the faults in this study are undoubtedly mine, I cannot lay sole claim to its strengths.

Writing and Reality: Contexts

The thing that he was about to do was to open a diary. This was
not illegal (nothing was illegal, since there were no longer any
laws), but if detected it was reasonably certain that it would be
punished by death, or at least by twenty-five years in a forced-
labour camp. Winston fitted a nib into the penholder and sucked it
to get the grease off. The pen was an archaic instrument, seldom
used even for signatures, and he had procured one, furtively and
with some difficulty, simply because of a feeling that the beautiful
creamy paper deserved to be written on with a real nib instead of
being scratched with an ink-pencil. Actually he was not used to
writing by hand. Apart from very short notes, it was usual to
dictate everything into the speakwrite, which was of course
impossible for his present purpose. He dipped the pen into the ink
and then faltered for just a second. A tremor had gone through his
bowels. To mark the paper was the decisive act. In small clumsy
letters he wrote:

April 4th, 1984

(Orwell, *Nineteen Eighty-Four*, p. 9)

Few, I imagine, would deny the present-day relevance of Winston
Smith's act of subversion; political prisoners throughout the world
continue to risk their lives by similar acts. But in one respect,
Winston Smith (or perhaps more correctly George Orwell) would be
envied by British writers today. What he writes is of less impor-

tance than the act of writing: "To mark the paper was the decisive act." In a society in which pen and paper are almost impossible to obtain, in a society in which all written records are those rewritten by the state, and in a society that manipulates thought by enforcing a state-controlled language, Winston Smith has merely to write down a possibly inaccurate date and already he has made a stand on the side of intellectual freedom: in *Nineteen Eighty-Four*, the idea of keeping a diary is a breach of Doublethink. Yet in a society that openly proclaims intellectual freedom and grants everyone the means to keep a diary, few will commence a diary with trembling bowels. What makes the modern fictive diarist hesitate is not so much fear of the Secret Police as a loss of belief in the connection between writing and reality, between text and the world. The prohibitions hanging over Winston Smith reinforce his belief that it is possible to write the truth, but, in a post-Saussurean world, it is no longer possible to believe quite so readily in the diary as documentary. Diary writing has lost its innocence.

If *Nineteen Eighty-Four* comes out of events of the 1930s and the 1940s, the violent political events of the 1950s in Eastern Europe provoked a new generation of left-wing British writers into taking up for themselves the Orwellian issue of individual freedom versus state coercion. Both Doris Lessing and John Berger used the diary like Orwell as a benchmark for individual freedom, but in both cases diary writing comes to be seen ultimately as an evasion of social responsibility. It may be a necessary step toward freedom, but it has to be relinquished in the face of political events. In Lessing's *The Golden Notebook* (1962), the diarist Anna Wulf explores the reality of her own life by keeping four separate notebooks. For her, the pressure of world events and political upheaval pose a threat to the very notion of individuality, and it is only after she has gone beyond words, gone beyond writing and come face to face with the terror underlying reality that she can overcome her sense of disintegration. Having testified to this experience in a single notebook, the Golden Notebook itself, Anna gives up diary writing, indeed she gives away her notebook, and reengages with society.

John Berger's *A Painter of Our Time* (1958) is a similar testament to the individual under stress by the political events of the 1950s, and, like Lessing's Anna Wulf, Berger's exiled Hungarian painter–diarist in the end must abandon his diary and return to social action, in his case to the Hungary of 1956. In both of these works, diary writing may accurately portray contemporary reality, may indeed act as an agent by which the diarist clarifies his or her own position, yet keeping a diary does not itself represent, as it does in Orwell, an act of political defiance. The diary has become too much of a refuge for a private, evasive self, too self-indulgent; for political action and a fuller sense of social responsibility, the diarist must pass into a world beyond the diary.

Put in the context of Lessing and Berger, Malcolm Lowry's "Through the Panama" (written largely in the early 1950s though not published until 1961) seems to epitomize this sterile self-indulgence since its main concern seems to be the shifting identity of the diarist who may or may not be Sigbjørn Wilderness, Martin Trumbaugh, or indeed Lowry himself. This introversion is matched by the technique of framing texts within texts, a technique that not only exceeds the very possibilities of the diary itself but questions the fundamental distinction between fact and fiction. Writing becomes a way of creating several alternative and conflicting realities without establishing any coherent dominant reality. If Orwell retains a belief in the ability of the diary to record reality, and Lessing and Berger retain this belief despite a growing unease about the innocence of language, Lowry abandons this belief altogether; selfhood dissolves and with it the possibility of political action.

Yet placing Lowry alongside Lessing highlights similarities as well as differences. In the way that Lowry's diarist is an amalgam of conflicting identities, so too is Lessing's Anna Wulf. And given that both diarists are also novelists, the discussion of identity is also a discussion of the dividing line between reality and art, fact and fiction. Both Lowry and Lessing use the diary strategy self-reflexively to examine the referential status of writing generally, and, while Lessing diverges from Lowry in arguing for a reality beyond words, such a position depends ultimately on a humanism she has apparently rejected and which cannot be demonstrated within the text. On the other hand, while Lowry and/or his diarist may be criticized for self-indulgence, the move beyond realism into the labyrinths of textuality has proved one of the most radical changes in the form of the novel in the twentieth-century, and one that Lessing, and indeed Berger, was not able to ignore.

The problem that emerges from the argument so far is, can the diary novel be used to discuss the relationship between writing and reality without saying either that there is no objective reality (Lowry) or that reality exists only beyond the text (Lessing)? In other words, where Lowry suggests that writing is a narcissistic conjuring with realities, both Lessing and Berger see diary writing only as a prelude to an active engagement with reality. In all three cases, writing is intransitive, is divorced from social action. An attempt to bridge the gap between Lowry and Lessing and justify writing as an Orwellian engagement with political reality can be seen in the 1960s and early 1970s in the work of B. S. Johnson.

Johnson was part of a group of young British writers working in London who looked toward Joyce and Beckett for a form of the novel which matched modern reality rather than to what they saw as an ossified nineteenth-century realism. In other words, in rejecting the literary practices of the cultural élite, they were consciously rejecting the values behind those practices. Johnson attempted to demonstrate the underlying chaos of reality by destroying the coherence of a realism that represented order and control. This ultimately posed unresolvable epistemological problems since it is impossible to demonstrate the chaos behind language using any form of signification; in any case, Johnson's aleatory strategies were always carefully contrived to allow his protagonists and his readers to come to the correct conclusions. Yet despite his deep suspicion of language, not only did Johnson not opt for Lessing's strategy of separating language from social action, he questioned the way the traditional realist creation of meaning through writing worked against the socially underprivileged. The realist novel was for Johnson the mouthpiece of the 1950s' cultural and political establishment, and, to the degree that realism endorsed the values of a political hierarchy, his view of writing as a way of manipulating thought is close to Orwell's: the privileging of certain types of discourse reinforce material power relationships; or as Johnson would have it, the establishment created a fiction (the realist novel) to be read as truth. Whereas in *Nineteen Eighty-Four* the writing of a diary is a subversive act against the endorsed language of the state, for Johnson, writing the experimental novel is an act of sabotage against a cultural and ideological élite. In *Travelling People* (1963), Johnson used the diary form along with letters, film scripts, and the authorial interruptions borrowed from the eighteenth-century novel to demonstrate the conventionality of realism and the discursive construction of reality; it is not possible to say which of the discourses is closer to reality since they gain their meaning by a differential relation to the other discourses. And in *Trawl* (1966), Johnson uses the periodicity of the diary form to represent a socially displaced working-class consciousness grappling to find the real meaning of events yet never quite overcoming the conventional discursive structuring of the chaos of reality.

Ann Quin and Eva Figes were both members of Johnson's circle in the late 1960s and, like Johnson, they used the diary strategy to examine the textuality of reality and, by implication, the cultural relativity of a humanist concept of self existing beyond discourse. Ann Quin's two novels that use the diary format, *Three* (1966) and *Passages* (1969), are particularly useful in that they show clearly the North American influence on the younger British writers of the time, the diaries representing the surrealism of contemporary reality seen from a mystically dispersed consciousness that became a hallmark of the so-called drug-culture. On the other hand, the challenge these British writers posed to the social realism of the traditional British novel also owed much to European influences—Beckett had already pursued the narrative imperatives of the diary form in *Malone Dies* (1951; translated 1956), and the influence of two of the most celebrated diary novels of the twentieth century, Sartre's *Nausea* (1938; translated 1949) and Michel Butor's *Passing Time* (1957; translated 1961), cannot be overlooked. Indeed, the influence of *Nausea* can be seen earlier in both *The Golden Notebook* and John Fowles's first published novel, *The Collector* (1963), half of which is in the form of a diary; both novels clearly take up the existentialist implications of diary writing.

In America, the influence of Sartre can be seen much earlier in Saul Bellow's first novel, *Dangling Man* (1944), where the hero experiences the "nausea" of an existentialist freedom in the period between resigning from his job and joining the army. But in contrast to the British experience, the diary form was not used during the 1960s and early 1970s by the experimental novelists. Diary novels continued to be written by notable American writers—witness Alison Lurie's *Real People* (1969) and John Updike's *A Month of Sundays* (1975)—but such novels did not radically question the diary's formal realism or its ability to transcribe a knowable reality; in the case of Lurie and Updike, the diary form is used to show that self-deception lies in the diarist and not in the world the diarist transcribes. Of the foremost American exponents of anti-realism in the 1960s and early 1970s, and one thinks here of such figures as John Barth, Thomas Pynchon, William Burroughs, Richard Brautigan, and Kurt Vonnegut, only Vonnegut in *Mother Night* (1961) made extended use of the diary format, a cultural difference from the British experience still to be explained.

By the later 1970s and with the advent in Britain of structuralist thinking, the possibility had been widely established through a systematic body of cultural theory that reality was not something that existed beyond the text but that it existed discursively, that it was relative and depended on the way in which a culture organized its discourses. This model then became a means by which writers like Eva Figes could explore the revitalized issue of women in society. In some ways works such as Eva Figes' *Nelly's Version* (1977) and Emma Tennant's *The Bad Sister* (1978) still contain within them the problematic that B. S. Johnson fought with, the degree to which an attack on realism could also be an attack on social inequality; in other words, the diary novel would seem to have to accept that realism accurately represents (an unjust) social reality and is more than a cultural convention. Nevertheless, by associating realism with a patriarchal view of the world, both Figes and Tennant are able to use the conventionality of realism to make a social point: in Figes, realism is undercut from within, the novel first accepting then rejecting the codes of realism, such as the discrete nature of characters (female characters merge) and the effacing of textuality (the novel itself appears within the novel); in Tennant, the realism of a (male) editorial frame fails to make sense of and contain the alternative female reality depicted by the diary within the frame.

British diary fiction in the 1980s, along with other areas of cultural production, has reacted against the formal experimentalism of the 1950s and 1960s and in so doing has moved back toward the tradition of realism. To be sure, Doris Lessing has produced a second work of diary fiction, *The Diaries of Jane Somers* (1984), yet while it repeats certain themes of *The Golden Notebook* it lacks their demonic stylistic force. And in the case of two other innovative writers of the 1950s, Iris Murdoch and William Golding, though both have, like Lessing, produced later works in the form of diary fiction, the fact that *The Sea, The Sea* (1978) and *Rites of Passage* (1980) both won the Booker McConnell prize suggests that neither poses a radical challenge to the sensibilities of the literary establishment. With regard to the other noted works of British diary fiction of the last decade, neither Robert Nye's *The Voyage of the Destiny* (1982) nor Margaret Forster's *Private Papers* (1986) can claim to represent a new departure for the novel to the same degree as earlier diary novels by Johnson, Quin, and Figes, all writers of the same generation as Nye and Forster.

In this general climate, few of the writers to have established themselves in the last ten years have written diary fiction. The exception is Jane Rogers with *The Ice Is Singing* (1987), a work that explores such contemporary concerns as child abuse, the women's movement, and care of the elderly, yet which in its analysis of the

relationship between writing and reality, to my mind, disappoint-
ingly echoes first *The Golden Notebook* and then B. S. Johnson. Its
final strategy, that of abandoning the diary for life itself, would
seem therefore to leave the field free to a resurgent social realism
and a belief in the freedom of the individual, marking the end of
radical attempts since Orwell's *Nineteen Eighty-Four* to question
not only how free the individual may be but to challenge the very
way in which the structure of society depends upon an unchallenge-
able, natural reality. If this indeed is the case, then the current
formal conservatism of diary fiction makes Winston Smith's act of
rebellious diary writing more pertinent than ever.

Initially, at least, the importance of post-war British diary fiction
rests on the canonical status of those British writers who have
used the diary form in their fiction. Works by Lessing, Golding,
Murdoch, Lowry, and Fowles are an important enough body of British fiction even without adding to the list works by B. S. Johnson,
Eva Figes, Robert Nye, and Emma Tennant. The fact, therefore,
that all these writers should write works in the form of a diary is of
itself a strong argument in favour of taking a specific look at modern British diary fiction. And it should not be forgotten that the two
greatest influences on British fiction in the twentieth century,
Joyce and Beckett, also toyed with the diary form: Joyce prefigured
the interior monologue of *Ulysses* (1922) and thence the extreme
textuality of *Finnegans Wake* (1939) in the diary sections at the end
of *A Portrait of the Artist as a Young Man* (1916); Beckett's disman-
tling of the diary form in *Malone Dies* has already been mentioned.

But what I would also argue is that, for two main reasons, it is not
just coincidence these writers have all toyed with diary fiction. The
first reason is that writing diary fiction, unlike writing novels
which efface their own textuality, allows writers to interrogate
something intrinsic to the novel, the novel as writing. What these
writers have done by foregrounding the textuality of the novel is to
interrogate the relationship between their writing and the reality
it aims to represent. In this sense, writing about writing, the self-
reflexive novel, has not proved as sterile as many would contend
and is an attempt to highlight writing as a cultural and social practice. Thus Patricia Waugh is able to argue that through metafiction, "far from 'dying,' the novel has reached a mature recognition
of its existence as *writing*, which can only ensure its continued
viability in and relevance to a contemporary world which is similarly beginning to gain awareness of precisely how its values and
practices are constructed and legitimized" (p. 19). The mention of

legitimization situates Waugh's study within the broad project of
cultural criticism, concerned less with the valorization of good literature than with the way in which all forms of discourse operate to
transmit or to challenge cultural values. The diary novel, it seems
to me, by placing a nonfiction form within quotations, as it were, is
well placed to challenge the assumptions lying behind writing as a
direct representation of a natural reality.

This leads on to the second reason why diary fiction has played
such a leading role in post-war British fiction. The nonfiction diary,
at least since Pepys was decoded and appropriated in 1825, has been
invested with a whole host of dominant cultural values. The diary
has come to encompass the first or leading term in a number of
cultural oppositions: conscience/ideology; private/public; sincerity/
convention; the individual/the mob; immediacy/artificiality; spon-
taneity/repression; formlessness/artifice; empiricism/theory; truth/
dogma. The diary in Western culture has developed from the historical chronicle, through private *aide-mémoire*, through puritan
confession, through romantic autobiography, to the *journal intime*
and the dream diary of psychoanalytic self-discovery. Written in
private for the diarist's eyes alone, the diary has accumulated in its
development a range of specific cultural values centered on the
concept of a unique and essentially rational human subject.

It is because of its investment with the values of a dominant
ideology that, in a period of rapid social change since the Second
World War, the diary has acted as a focus for cultural introspection.
My task, therefore, is to examine through an interrogation of the
diary as discourse the ways in which modern British diary fiction
has questioned cultural values, has questioned the way the diary
has been used to legitimate certain cultural values. To this end and
rather than giving an amplified chronological survey, I shall be
concentrating on specific areas of contestation: facticity, history,
autobiography, and gender. The following two chapters act as a
necessary theoretical prelude to this project and may be omitted in
a first reading should the reader be impatient to engage with my
analysis of the texts themselves: Chapter 2 discusses the issues
involved in normative attempts to define the nonfiction diary, to
police its boundaries, and to invest the diary form with cultural
values, while Chapter 3 considers the broader issue of how cultural
distinctions between fact and fiction interact with formal distinctions between the nonfiction and the fictive diary. Chapter 4 deals
with the commonsense assumption that the diary records the raw
material of reality and examines how this assumption depends on a

fundamentally unstable relationship between different types of discourse. Chapter 5 deals with the diary as historical chronicle and, in the light of contemporary historiography, considers the ways in which modern diary novels have undermined the objectivity of the discourse of history and negotiated the meaning of public events. Chapter 6 looks at how diary fiction has contested the autobiographical assumptions behind diary writing, the diary as the sanctuary of a discrete narratorial selfhood, and offers instead a selfhood that is the result of a dialectic between different subject positions. In Chapter 7, I consider a spectrum of modern treatments of the oldest type of European diary fiction, the fictive sea journal, to show the degrees to which writers are prepared to question cultural values through their treatment of the diary as document; and, in Chapter 8, I consider the ways in which the cultural association of women with diaries has been appropriated by women writers to reappraise the representation of female identity and the way in which gender differences are literally written into the structure of society. In the concluding chapter, I offer an overview of the range of formal strategies used by modern British diary fiction to interrogate the cultural relationship between discourses.

From the preceding, it can be seen that this study has a dual focus. First, to the degree that it is a study of diary fiction it aims to outline the possibilities opened by developments in British writing over the last thirty years or so. It thus pays most attention to works that question the traditional codes of realism through a modernist use of a deep and an often arbitrary symbolic structure but also and more particularly through a postmodern preoccupation with the text as writing, what I have already referred to as the textuality of reality. In other words, the present study will itself privilege the self-referential, experimental text over works of literary realism on the understanding that their interrogation of the diary is necessarily an interrogation of the humanist assumptions concerning the notion of a self beyond discourse that are invested in the diary.

It is, of course, arguable that even traditional realist diary fiction is preoccupied with writing and its problematic relationship to reality because the diary itself is a written text; diary novels are always implicated as writing. Yet for my purposes I would want to make a distinction between the problems of transcribing a reality the meaning of which is assumed to exist independently of the writing and the realization that written discourses are a social practice which actively constitute reality. In other words, the problem I am interested in is not so much how to capture an extra-textual or social reality on the page but how to interrogate the relationship between discourses by which certain values are culturally enforced. To the degree that Western culture privileges the personal, the sincere, the spontaneous, and the artless, this necessarily involves disrupting such seemingly natural and certainly comforting divisions as those between autobiography and fiction, history and the novel, and the private and the public. The conventions of the classic realist text, such as unified characters, recognizable settings, narrative closure, and authorial overview, restrict the extent to which realist diary fiction is able to foreground its own textuality.

Side by side with this focus on modernist and postmodern texts that question the conventions of realism, the approach I adopt to the study of diary fiction biases my study in favour of those texts that are most responsive to an approach through the formal analysis of linguistic style and narrative structure. In other words, my methodology is that of a reader-orientated structuralist analysis of narrative overlayed with a poststructuralist critique of the writing subject and a historicist notion of culture as the site of conflicting ideological discourses. This, in itself, privileges an analysis of text over any representation of reality that effaces textuality and is, it has to be admitted, most at home with formally experimental works. However, since the development of the novel over the past thirty or forty years has been contemporary with the development of the critical practices I adopt, it is hardly surprising that the relationship of writing to reality should be of importance to both novelist and critic alike. The two inhabit a common culture, a common set of discursive practices. As Malcolm Bradbury has said of structuralism, "it has afforded a method for the examination of the constitutive processes by which we generate reality, seek to compose communally an agreed and shareable world" ("Modern Literary Theory," p. 137). With the proviso that there never can be and never should be an agreed and shareable world (apart from the fact that it would always marginalize some group somewhere, it would be extremely boring), I take this convergence of interest in writing as a constitutive process as a strength rather than a weakness, conceding that the texts I write about may be read and evaluated differently by those with different interests, yet believing that where my readings may appear contentious they do have merit in debating the texts through the problematics of their own time.

2

Policing the Boundaries

CAN THE DIARY BE DEFINED?

To say that this or that diary novel imitates the nonfiction diary to
this or that degree is to imply that there is some model of the diary
to be imitated. To demonstrate an imitation of form would be impossible without being able to specify certain features characteristic of the form being imitated. For example, to say that a given
diary is too artfully composed to be a real diary is to draw on a
convention of the diary as an unshaped record, that in a real
diary the diarist is not concerned with composing an organized
narrative. In turn, we would need to translate this convention into
formal features such as thematic development or type of sentence
structure in order to demonstrate our case. Yet it is almost a tru-
ism of studies of both the nonfiction diary and the diary novel that
the texts themselves exceed the possibility of homogeneity. Each
convention we may describe as a convention of the diary is either
not maintained by all diaries or is found in other types of writing.

If we take first the nonfiction diary, K. Eckhard Kuhn-Osius
demonstrates in a particularly clear analysis of a body of German
diaries how the texts themselves exceed attempts to trace a unify-
ing element: "It is very difficult to say anything about diaries
which is true for all of them" ("Making Loose Ends Meet," p. 166).
Hence:

. . . the content of a diary cannot be predicted or made the touchstone of its diaristic qualities. (p. 166)

One might mention a certain regularity of entries—but that is more hope than observation. (p. 166)

. . . diaries have first-person narrator and point of view. But they are different from first-person fictional stories and from letters or essays. This distinction is perfectly clear in theory, although the specifics of an individual text may be difficult to deal with in practice. (p. 167)

The differences between diarist and novelist cannot be ascertained on the basis of a simple true/false or fact/fiction dichotomy. (p. 167)

The diary is not [addressed to someone other than the diarist]—at least, not necessarily. (p. 167)

What Kuhn-Osius does pinpoint in the diary is a tendency toward both plotlessness, which is derived from the diarist's position within the passage of time, and indeterminacy, namely, the existence of gaps in the text arising from presuppositions held by the diarist but not shared by the reader. But even if we agree with this, notions of plotlessness and indeterminacy produce only poles between which actual diaries may shift, according to the degree they admit readers other than the diarist. In short, the diary may be more or less private according to the extent to which the diarist is concerned with "making loose ends meet."

In the case of the diary novel, Gerald Prince has tried in "The Diary Novel" to locate features that permit a definition of the fictive diary as a sub-genre of the novel. Again, though, the possibility of variants undermines any formal definition drawn from the texts themselves:

. . . it is not a superficial journal shape which particularizes a diary novel . . . because some well-known diary novels do not adopt that exterior shape. (p. 477)

. . . some first-person novels which exhibit the superficial features of a journal and come fully equipped with dates as section headings are often not thought of as diary novels. (p. 477)

. . . many first-person novels the narrator of which is also the main character are not fictive diaries. (p. 477)

. . . in the diary novel, the narration is fragmented, as it were, and inserted between various sequences of events. A diary novel always implies several narrative occasions. . . . This characteristic mode of narration, however, is not found in diary novels only. Epistolary novels too provide good examples. (p. 478)

. . . although many fictitious diarists seem to be writing for themselves only, many also write for other readers. (p. 478)

Prince's conclusion is that "The narrative techniques resulting from the journal form, though they characterize diary novels to a certain extent, do not therefore set them apart from all other fiction" (p. 479). What does set the diary novel apart as a sub-genre of the novel, Prince suggests, is not any particular narrative technique but rather "the theme of writing a diary and its concomitant themes and motifs" (p. 479). In other words, unlike other types of fiction the diary novel is concerned with such matters as why the diarist keeps a diary, what keeping a diary means to the narrator, where and when the diary is written, what its physical form is, and how it came to be published.

Both Prince and Kuhn-Osius demonstrate the difficulty of defining the formal characteristics of the diary by describing a group of texts, and the lesson would seem to be that attempts to define the diary will inevitably be counterproductive. Any definition will be prescriptive since a description of diaries produces contradictory results, actual texts always exceeding the bounds of a definition. However, the alternative—to abandon the whole notion of a formal definition of the diary as a genre—is a more dangerous option; the freedom such a move allows is the freedom to be even more narrowly prescriptive.

A case in point is Robert Fothergill's *Private Chronicles: A Study of English Diaries*. Fothergill begins his study at a point similar to that arrived at by Prince, defining the diary not by consideration of formal criteria but according to a flexible notion of usage: "In general let it be agreed that a diary is what a person writes when he says, 'I am writing my diary'" (p. 3). Yet by sidestepping the whole question of generic form, Fothergill produces a study of diaries that actually dismisses works which most readers would find typical of the genre: "The great mass of diary-writing is poor stuff, interesting only to the antiquarian or the social historian" (p. 2). In other words, by ignoring primary questions of definition, Fothergill is able to concentrate on such secondary and atypical criteria as "serial autobiography" and "the book of the self," criteria that place a high value on certain notions of the writer's personality and the text's thematic unity. Thus "a study of English diaries" becomes in practice a study of a highly prescriptive notion of the literary diary.

As Fothergill himself admits: "The case for undertaking a study of English diary-writing rests upon the extraordinary character and distinction of a handful of examples" (p. 1). The case of the ordinary diary has been judicially dismissed as "poor stuff."

Fothergill's position might be more convincing had he taken into account his own presuppositions. Fothergill believes that his handful of examples "insist on being prized" (p. 2), arguing that "The business of asserting a 'great tradition' of English diary-writing is inseparable from the effort to formulate the criteria that systematically express this 'greatness'" (p. 2). The assertion of a Great Tradition is, though, a cultural practice, a way of reading texts according to certain literary values, and while such a project is valid to the degree that it is conscious of its own method, what the Great Tradition does not do is innocently order texts according to some inherent greatness. Fothergill succeeds, therefore, in merely proving that those texts he selected for their greatness display precisely those criteria he uses to define greatness, namely, those literary values he associates with the Great Tradition. The conclusion must be that while any study of diary writing might plausibly group together texts according to some common factor, we should not forget it is we as readers who choose, consciously or unconsciously, which particular taxonomy we impose. Certainly there is nothing in Fothergill's *Private Chronicles* that leads us to dispute the findings of Prince or Kuhn-Osius that no definition of the diary describes the entire field of actual diary writing.

What is clear from Fothergill's study is that our choice of a body of texts may also bring with it other factors which influence our findings. It is obvious, for instance, that Fothergill's decision to use only published diaries has magnified his results. Although only a tenth of his texts were written this century, nearly all were published after 1900, and it is likely most were chosen for publication precisely because they conformed to the same literary values that underpin his own critical position. In other words, the publishing climate this century has privileged and, despite some academic opposition, seems set to continue to privilege the literary memoir because of both its structural coherence and its ethos of the exceptional personality.

This situation is complicated by additional factors such as libel laws. Few nonfiction diaries are either published or made available immediately on the death of the diarist, and living diarists are unlikely to part in any great number with their manuscripts. Thus, if like Fothergill and Kuhn-Osius we wish to study the nonfiction diary for defining characteristics, we are necessarily forced to study works of earlier periods. And since one of the objects of such a study would be to locate shifts in technique, we would be precluded from observing any contemporary shifts, the effect, let us presume, of Sue Townsend's best-selling *The Secret Diary of Adrian Mole* on subsequent diary writing.

Turning to fictive diaries, the main concern of the present study, we might expect to find a more amenable situation. In terms of defining the diary by analyzing a body of contemporary texts, there is not the time lag that exists in the case of nonfiction diaries between composition and reading, and we might hope to find some homogeneity among texts written in the past twenty years or so. Prince deals with works covering a time span from 1850 to 1966, and over such a period we might predict if not major then at least some minor changes in diary conventions. But even with a contemporary body of diary novels there are two other complicating factors.

The first is that the development of diary fiction does not necessarily parallel developments in the nonfiction diary. For example, Lorna Martens in *The Diary Novel* points out that in the late eighteenth century there arose the hybrid form of the letter-journal, fictive diaries which were addressed to a specific addressee (p. 76). Thus the diary novel borrowed not only from the nonfiction diary but also from the novel, specifically from the epistolary novel. And this today has become a resource of modern diary fiction. Moreover, we have to be extremely careful to assess where the diary novel is imitating not the nonfiction diary but the diary novel itself—certainly in the case of parody, the model may be novelistic rather than nonfictional, and where the diary novel exhibits the plotlessness associated with the nonfiction diary it is likely to be read, as I argue later, as an anti-novel rather than as a strict imitation of a nonfiction model.

This leads on to the second factor which complicates our defining the diary from a body of contemporary diary fiction. Contemporary diary novels may well be influenced by current self-reflexive trends in the novel which do not necessarily affect the contemporary nonfiction diary. To be sure, diaries have for long had the potential for being self-reflexive, for thematizing the very act of writing, yet the degree to which such reflexivity is the same as that found in the modern novel is open to question. Self-reflexiveness may differ according to the proposed relationship between writing and reality.

It seems, then, that contemporary diary fiction is likely to be as diverse as Prince concludes his whole range of diary novels to be, and, coupling his findings with those of Kuhn-Osius, we have to conclude that it is impossible to arrive at a stable notion of the diary from an analysis of either nonfiction diaries or diary novels. While any specific work may be concerned with the practice of diary writing, an analysis of a body of such works will for numerous reasons undermine the relatively clear criteria by which we can label such works as diaries in the first place. Might it not be better, therefore, to talk not in terms of the diary, with its generic implications, but in terms of diary writing? The answer is "yes" if that means we are able to include works that are not labeled diaries and so avoid imposing fixed borders on our field of study. Yet the answer must also be "no" insofar as we return to our original problem, namely, the problem of specifying the degree to which a work adopts or subverts our notion of a diary. We must of course scrutinize the basis of the closure we impose, particularly if we are to avoid the prescriptive procedures of Fothergill. Yet any study of the way in which diary fiction contests the values underlying the diary must necessarily adopt some criteria in order to proceed at all. Some attempt at a definition must be made.

The resolution of what amounts to a clash between theory and empiricism resides not in the one or the other but in the relationship between the two. For the attempt to define the diary by an analysis of texts, even if the attempt fails, is itself already founded on some prior notion of what constitutes a diary. In other words, a definition precedes the investigation in the very choice of which features should be investigated. And the strength of such a definition resides in the fact that it relies neither on a manipulation of actual texts into a preconceived taxonomy nor on the demonstrably difficult task of arriving at a definition solely by investigating actual texts (as in Kuhn-Osius and Prince). Rather the definition resides in the mind of the reader as he or she evaluates an actual text. Thus, while both Kuhn-Osius and Prince admit the existence of degrees to which a work may or may not live up to expectations of the diary form, this in itself is based upon a number of prior assumptions as to what constitutes a diary. For instance, the text may be addressed to someone other than the diarist, but this is notable only if we expect diarists to write solely for themselves. Such criteria precede the analysis of the works and, even if all the diaries we came across contained an addressee, we would as readers still find this remarkable since it ran counter to our expectations of diary conventions. As readers, we (and by that I mean fairly literate Western readers) expect diaries to be written solely for the diarist.

What then are these presuppositions which underpin a reading of diary writing? The following are those criteria against which Kuhn-Osius (in "Making Loose Ends Meet") implicitly tested his actual texts:

1. the diary has a first-person narrator and point of view (p. 167);
2. the diary is written in instalments corresponding to the time of composition (p. 166);
3. the entries do not constitute a unity of action (p. 169);
4. the diarist writes for himself or herself (p. 167);
5. the diary contains areas of indeterminacy (p. 171).

This last point, the areas of indeterminacy, results from the real reader not sharing exactly the knowledge of someone writing only for himself or herself (point 4).

Using Prince ("The Diary Novel"), we can abstract a second implicit definition:

1. the diary is a first-person text in which the narrator is the protagonist in the events he or she records (p. 477);
2. there are a certain number of sections each preceded by a more or less specific date (p. 477);
3. the narration is fragmented, inserted between various sequences of events (p. 478);
4. the diarist writes only for himself or herself (p. 478).

These four criteria are almost identical with those of Kuhn-Osius and there is a high degree of correlation between the two sets of presuppositions. Despite their findings, therefore, Kuhn-Osius and Prince begin their studies with a common idea of what constitutes a diary.

Now, insofar as actual diaries may be in the second or third grammatical person, may or may not be dated, may be to a greater or lesser extent periodic, and may even be written for a range of addressees from a friend to the public at large, it needs to be asked how the norm against which these appear as variants is sustained. It is tempting to say that there is a basic model from which the more literate or self-consciously literary diarists depart, yet such an explanation is founded on a dubious equation of cultural hierarchy with literary sophistication, and it is not borne out by examination of such a complex work as the diary of Hannah Cullwick, a Victorian domestic servant who had no developed literacy.

My own suggestion is that the diary norm is attached to the word *diary* and exists as a cultural paradigm or model separate from diary writing as a practice. In this case, it would not be at all surprising that the practice not only differed from the model but did so necessarily. Certainly Lorna Martens has demonstrated that the history of the word *diary* is very different from the history of those traits we find in diary writing today, stating that the word diary has in the past denoted "retrospective first-person narratives and impersonal predictive texts (almanacs). . . . sometimes it has signified chiefly a particular kind of content" (*The Diary Novel*, p. 27). I am aware here that Martens is not directly accounting for the kind of distinction I am suggesting between the traits associated with the diary as a concept and those found in diary-writing practice, yet her comments usefully underline the play of historical changes which is continually postponing any synchronic identity between word and practice. Genre classifications are not Platonic ideals fixed for all time. Moreover, Martens does seem to accept the distinction between the word and its practice when she talks of the "signification" of the word *diary*: "Its signification at a given time often, in fact usually, has a determining influence on the form, style, and content of what the author of a diary novel writes" (p. 27). To the degree that this signification is only an influence and thus separable from the practice of diary writing, as Kuhn-Osius has shown it is not only the diary novel but the nonfiction diary that is flexible in form, style, and content.

My point, then, is that for contemporary Western readers there is a paradigm of the diary which exists separate from the texts we refer to as diaries, and that the paradigm and its associated traits are attached to the word *diary*. Hence the possibility of a dictionary definition. Similarly, the concept of a *journal* (as a literary document) or a *chronicle* (as a historical document) exists separate from what in practice we call journals or chronicles where the distinction from the *diary* becomes untenable. Thus, the norm that we use to gauge the degree to which a work may or may not be a diary is sustained as a cultural concept, that is, as a paradigm shared by a certain community of readers. Indeed, it is arguable that the sharing of such genre paradigms helps to define a culture, being built, as I argue below, upon certain privileged values. On the one hand, therefore, we might conjecture in the abstract that it is not necessary to have written or even have read a diary in order to know what a diary is. On the other hand, a work that does not in practice adopt all the criteria associated with the word *diary* is not necessarily not labeled a diary.

Before I go on to examine the actual textual features by which we recognize diary traits, I want briefly to examine certain implications of the position we have now reached. In particular I seem to be suggesting that the notion of a diary as a genre is based not so much on the actual practice of diary writing but upon an abstract and prescriptive definition. I must stress again, therefore, that actual diaries may exceed such a definition and yet remain recognizably diaries: neither Kuhn-Osius nor Prince was questioning that the works under consideration were diaries, only that there seemed to be no predictable common features. The consequence of this, however, is to appear to reject the notion of a cognitive oscillation by which we as readers move from expectations to text and then back to our expectations in order to revise them. Such a process of referral and adjustment usefully accounts for the way in which a specific reader reading a specific text is able both to interpret the text and to develop a knowledge of genres; it also partially accounts for the way in which generic definitions themselves develop in the light of changes in literary practice. Clearly the wholesale rejection of such a process would be difficult to sustain, and what we now have to consider is why a work may break from the paradigm and yet still be called a diary.

First, it is possible to show that a text may itself signal its departure from a feature of the paradigm by some sort of contract with the reader. The title of Enid Bagnold's *A Diary Without Dates* is a good example of the way a text can revoke its adherence to the paradigm, in this case by the omission of the dateline. More locally, a work can insert a disclaimer in an individual diary entry, as in the diary of Joe Orton where he draws attention to lapses in the regularity of his diary keeping due to illness or pressures of work: "*Saturday 14 January* [1967]. Felt better today. Spent this morning writing up the events of the last few days" (p. 62); "*Sunday 5 February* [1967]. Very badly kept journal of the last few days" (p. 78). The point about such disclaimers is that they acknowledge and reinforce generic expectations, a point I take up in the following chapter with regard to diary fiction.

Second, it is also possible to account for this disparity between model and text by reference to the notion of literary competence.

The notion of literary competence was first suggested by Jonathan Culler in *Structuralist Poetics* using an analogy with Chomsky's notion of linguistic competence (p. 9). While linguistic competence refers to the language user's implicit knowledge of the underlying rules of language, literary competence refers to the reader's ability to understand the second-order system of literature and genre. This analogy is to some extent misleading in that, as has been pointed out by Nigel Fabb and Alan Durant, language acquisition is an innate process whereas the internalization of generic rules is the result of a specialized form of learning ("Ten Years On," p. 53). Nevertheless, the analogy is useful in that it allows us to distinguish between competence and performance, between the model and the employment of the model. As Culler himself points out, the model is not exhausted by its manifestations but is rather a system of rules of what is possible (p. 9). Moreover, performance may violate the rules and still be understood by reference to the rules—the sort of violation, in fact, I have just pointed to in Orton. In short, the existence of a generic paradigm aids cognition but is not necessarily narrowly prescriptive.

Finally, however, we need to see the diary as just one of a whole matrix of possible genre classifications. The diary is linked, for example, to the memoir, the letter, the commonplace book, and the confession, and given the dynamics of literary evolution as traced in the diary by Martens, the boundaries between genres will not be easily delimited but will be areas of interaction, contestation, and ultimately of indeterminacy. Moreover, the change in the configuration of one genre will affect the configuration of those features associated with related genres. Here it becomes evident that we are talking of wider cultural and social factors rather than strictly literary ones. And given the historical development of the paradigm and its consequent flexibility, we may do better, therefore, to talk less in terms of rules, as in Culler, and more in terms of a flexible configuration of features that individually may be found in other genres. Kuhn-Osius raises this possibility with reference to Wittgenstein: "To define the term 'diary,' one would have to start from a Wittgensteinian theory of *Familienähnlichkeiten* and assume that many traits belong to the diary but that not all diaries have all of them all of the time" ("Making Loose Ends Meet," p. 166). Kuhn-Osius himself rejects this because of the number of features involved; yet these are not in fact that numerous and what I want to do now is precisely to list those potential features which are included in the paradigm of the diary. The difficulty lies in specifying

which combinations of features result in a work still being classified as a diary. However, there are still strong enough reasons for
the limited undertaking I propose, not least of which is that it enables us to talk in terms of a diary novel as an imitation of a nonfiction diary, to recognize where a work is subverting the paradigm,
and to turn, as I do in the following chapter, to the textual differences between fact and fiction.

DESCRIBING THE PARADIGM

The following is a summary of the criteria of a diary paradigm
compiled from the assumptions of two experienced diary readers,
Kuhn-Osius and Prince. I will group these features under the over-
lapping headings of narrator, narration (that is, the way in which
the subject matter is narrated), and addressee:

Narrator: The diary is a first-person narration in which the narrator is
  also the protagonist; the recording is therefore from the narrator's
  point of view.
Narration: The diary is composed of regular dated sections corresponding
  to the time of composition; it has thus a fragmented narrative
  structure and is nonretrospective.
Addressee: The diarist is writing for himself or herself, the resultant style
  being abbreviated and containing semantic gaps.

To the extent that this paradigm is not derived from the actual
texts studied, I am suggesting that this is a norm associated with
the word *diary* rather than being drawn from diary practice. This
position is reinforced by the similarity of the working definitions
given by Lorna Martens, Valerie Raoul, and William Matthews in
three other works on diary writing:

. . . a first-person narrative that the narrator writes at periodic intervals
and essentially for himself. (Martens, *The Diary Novel*, p. 4)

The narrator writes in the first person, mainly about himself and primarily for himself. He writes "au jour le jour," that is, his account is concerned mainly with the recent past and the "present" of narration, the
future is unknown to him as he writes. He produces a written account, the
journal. (Raoul, *The French Fictional Journal*, p. 3)

. . . a personal record of what interested the diarist, usually kept day be
day, each day's record being self-contained and written soon after the
events occurred, the style usually being free from organised exposition.
(Matthews, *British Diaries*, p. xv)

It ought to be pointed out, however, that Martens in making her definition adds a qualification: "By assessing the empirical evidence in a fairly impressionistic way, we have arrived at a definition of what might be regarded as the *ideal* characteristics of the genre" (p. 6). I myself am not at all sure to what degree these "ideal" characteristics are in fact drawn from empirical evidence rather than from a preconceived idea of what constitutes a diary, but I accept that the normative or ideal nature of the definition must be handled with caution and that the departure from any feature of the norm does not necessarily preclude a work from being a diary. Moreover, as I stressed above, we know that such a definition may not hold for all periods of diary writing—I am concerned here only with the contemporary situation. Yet I would question Martens when she says, "it must be stressed that our provisional definition does not give us a criterion for deciding whether any given work is a diary novel or not" (p. 6). Like Prince and Kuhn-Osius, Martens goes on to point out how certain twentieth-century diary works depart from one or other criteria yet remain to some degree a diary; yet also like Prince and Kuhn-Osius to do so she relies on her ideal diary in order to locate areas of flexibility. Thus considering only retrospective narration, Martens states that Thomas Mann's *Doktor Faustus* "could not be considered a diary," that Gerhart Hauptmann's *Phantom* "is a borderline case," and that John Updike's *Month of Sundays* and François Mauriac's *Le Nœud de vipères* "are more diarylike" (pp. 6–7). In other words, such judgements depend on testing the text against all the criteria and assessing their relative importance and the degree to which they are adhered to. Certainly William Matthews feels confident enough in his own definition to use it to exclude from his bibliography of diaries, "travel narratives which are not day-by-day records, chronicles, commonplace books, ships' logs (though not diaries kept at sea, which seem to me to have a significant personal element), reminiscences, autobiographies, minutes, accounts, muster rolls, memoirs, all of which are sometimes called journals by their editors and publishers" (p. xv).

Despite its normative bias, then, we need a paradigm of the type outlined above in order to make statements about actual texts. Yet given the formal flexibility of actual diary writing, it needs again to be stressed that the division of texts into diaries or some other type of writing will depend on the individual configuration of the text under consideration and how consistent it is. It might seem, for instance, that the need for a text to be divided into a number of sections is an absolute criterion of the diary, but though a work with no divisions may be seen variously as a memoir, self-portrait, or essay, other texts such as historical analyses or collections of letters may contain chronological divisions without being diaries. And even within the individual criteria I have discussed above, a text may be, say, periodic or in the first person to a greater or lesser degree. The paradox, then, is that the diary depends on a precise model and yet in practice each work will have an individual configuration and an individual emphasis, a paradox that results in the failure of both Kuhn-Osius and Prince to define the diary by analyzing actual diaries. At best such a method might hope to produce a system of rules that can account for some of the various combinations of diary features, but without care it will only produce a potentially infinite set of descriptions of every possible configuration, a diversity that will become more apparent with the comparison of actual texts in later chapters.

THE VALUE-ADDED APPROACH

So far I have been careful to refer to the diary *form*, that is, to its linguistic style and narrative structure. This has been made possible by the fact that Kuhn-Osius, Prince, Martens, and Raoul are also careful to avoid certain value judgements, the pitfalls of which were seen in Fothergill's study where his criteria were at once held to select and to derive from the texts in a self-validating circle. However, it must not be forgotten that the development of the diary is not arbitrary and that the configuration of textual strategies that comprise the diary are validated through reference to cultural values. In other words, ideology plays a formative role in the development of genre. Some allowance, therefore, has to be made for what I will call the value-added approach if only because to ignore value judgements is to seem to accept them as a free-floating alternative to the approach through form. On the contrary, what I want to suggest is that though value judgements belong to the ideological field, they are firmly attached to the formal aspects of the text and play some part in our assessment of a diary. For example, to say that a norm of the diary is that the diarists write only for themselves is to expect to find an abbreviated style and a fragmented structure; conversely, a discursive style and unified structure suggest that the diary has been written for publication, and this becomes translatable as a suspicion that the diarist is not being truthful, that the diarist is being less than candid. Our current

cultural norm thus privileges the *private* diary, and such values
are functionally important particularly in the diary novel where an
ideological questioning of such humanist values as self-discovery
and sincerity come into play. Descriptive analysis in such cases
must recognize associated cultural values.

In terms of the *narrator*, the formal norm of the grammatical
first person privileges the individual, that is, the personality or
character of the diarist. Since the narrator is also the protagonist
the diary is also concerned with autobiography or, as Fothergill
would have it, "serial autobiography." We extrapolate a personality
from what a person does. And given that the diary is written from
the diarist's point of view, we are able to compare what the diarist
does with what he or she says to make judgements about the writer's sincerity.

So far as the *narration* is concerned, it is the moment rather
than the self that is privileged. A sense of the unselfconscious truth
is derived from the necessity of composing from day to day without
benefit of retrospection—the diarist is caught up in the imperative
of events. The fragmented narrative structure does not allow the
diarist to impose a unified pattern on the immediacy of day-to-day
life. It is precisely for this reason that our formal norm cannot
include a prior assumption of content, though there would be suspicion of a diary that did not include the domestic details of everyday life. The content should be mundane, giving an "authentic"
picture of daily living.

To turn to the *addressee* of the work, how far diarists write only
for themselves is also an index of the sincerity of the diarist, the
public or joint diary being devalued as a document of self-revelation.
And as H. Porter Abbott among others points out, diarists may
deceive themselves, be insincere, yet this is still a mark of authenticity in the diary, the diary as an authentic record of character
(*Diary Fiction*, p. 21). In addition, the existence of an abbreviated
style and semantic gaps to be found in the personal diary reinforces
that immediacy or freshness derived from daily composition.

Evidence for such readings can be found in the claims of a wide
range of diary commentators writing in the first half of the twentieth century, as might be gauged from a typical passage from
Arthur Ponsonby's *English Diaries* (1923):

Even the writer with little natural power of literary expression may scribble down a phrase at the moment which no amount of studied ingenuity
on the part of a literary author could equal. This spontaneity is a form of

sincerity which may be claimed as the one indispensable quality for a good diary. (p. 33)

The code words here are "scribble," "the moment," "spontaneity," and "sincerity," impressionistic terms which are held to distinguish the good diary, but which say nothing whatsoever about the formal attributes of the text. A second example of this type of commentary comes from P. A. Spalding's *Self-Harvest: A Study of Diaries and the Diarist* (1949): "The little incidents of daily life, provided that they are directly observed and instantly recorded, survive with a wonderful freshness" (pp. 26–27). The more one reads of such impressionistic commentaries, the more it becomes apparent that words such as "sincerity," "authenticity," "immediacy," and "truth" are at base predicated on two prime and mutually defining values, the primacy of the self and the primacy of the living moment: the diary reveals the true self as it spontaneously records the immediacy of the living moment. Thus the true self is guaranteed by being able to portray the living moment, while the portrayal of the living moment is guaranteed by being recorded by the true self. In short, we are dealing here with precisely that pervasive metaphysics of presence, the notion of being as presence, that Derrida finds underpinning Western ways of thinking about self, writing, and meaning.

My point, therefore, is that we must view such culturally specific evaluations with caution since they are relative rather than, as the commentators would have us believe, universal. However, some allowance must be made for these values, not only because they are traditionally associated with all diary writing, but because they account for the continuance of the diary form, since any form of writing rises and falls by its assimilation into a wider, if dominant, cultural system of values. The confession, for example, both religious and criminal, has long since gone out of fashion; the commonplace book has more recently disappeared. Moreover, even where diary writing seeks to subvert the metaphysics of presence, in the absence of an alternative system it must do so by deconstructing from within. We must be aware of the paradigm of the diary with its associated values in order to be aware of the ways in which modern British diary writing has challenged those values through formal experimentation. If I have drawn attention to the way the boundaries have been policed, it is not to concur with those boundaries but rather to show their cultural relativity and as a prelude to investigating how they have been challenged.

To avoid what I consider to be the pitfalls of the value-added approach, my own approach, as may have become apparent, will make continued reference to the reader rather than to the author of either the diary novel or the nonfiction diary. In other words, sincerity, truth, and self-revelation will refer to effects identified by the reader from consideration of the formal aspects of the text alone. These are not statements that refer to any specific conditions of production or which need verification in any extra-textual world. Neither am I restricting my reader to the position of any narratee, real or fictive, nor to any addressee silently implied by the text. Again these are textual effects to be observed rather than shared by the actual reader.

Of course, such a closure begs the question of which reader has the power to dictate the reading. Recent theorists have suggested many types of reader—Superreader, Implied Reader, Informed Reader, and Model Reader—yet what these terms demonstrate is the range of possible reading practices rather than any metatextual criterion by which a text might be analyzed. Such may be the case here; there is no metareader and other readings must surely coexist. However, in mitigation I would point out that wherever possible I try to account for the observations of identifiable readers, as in my discussion of formal assumptions above where I used Kuhn-Osius, Prince, Martens, and Raoul, and as in my analysis of the value-judgements of the diary commentators where I used Ponsonby and Spalding as representative examples. In other words, I employ the various and sometimes contradictory assumptions of a specific reading community, a community which may read and keep diaries. On the other hand, since I myself have been socialized into that culture, my readings of individual texts can rely ultimately on myself as my reader, providing, of course, I am conscious of the cultural construction of that perspective and am prepared to challenge it. Here, as in a great many other places, I follow Philippe Lejeune in his work on autobiography:

With regard to the text, I am adopting the reader's point of view: my starting point is neither the problematic internal state of the author, nor an attempt to establish the canons of a literary genre. By choosing to start from the situation of the reader (which is my own, the only one I know well), I may be able to grasp the functioning of the texts more clearly (and the differences in how they function), since they were written for us their readers, and since, as we read them, it is we who cause them to function. ("The Autobiographical Contract," pp. 192–93)

3

Diary Fact/Diary Fiction

LEJEUNE AND THE AUTOBIOGRAPHICAL PACT

In Carmarthen Public Library, there are two texts which are in the form of a diary but which are nonetheless categorized very differently on the shelves. *The Master Eccentric: The Journals of Rayner Heppenstall* is marked as nonfiction and shelved under biography, while *The Diaries of Jane Somers*, though bearing a similar title and consisting likewise of periodic entries, is classified as fiction. If we can assume that the agent who selects in which category to place a particular text does so using cognitive procedures open to the general reader, the question then becomes: on what basis is such a distinction made, what is there about two such texts which, despite obvious similarities, sets them stacks apart?

Philippe Lejeune, to whose work any study of the autobiographical genres ought to make reference, argues that the distinction between autobiography and fiction depends upon the identity of the author. The crucial condition is whether or not the protagonist of the work (who is also the narrator in autobiographies and diaries) is also the author whose name appears on the title page: "For there to be autobiography (and more generally *littérature intime*), there must be identity between the *author*, the *narrator*, and the *protagonist*" ("The Autobiographical Contract," p. 193). In the case of diaries, then, the diarist who is by definition both narrator and

protagonist must also be the book's author for the work to be classified as nonfiction.

Of course, this position is both a little idealistic and somewhat
normative, as Lejeune himself acknowledges in a re-reading of his
own study ["Le Pacte Autobiographique (bis)"]; but as he reminds
us there, one has to start somewhere, and his is a useful and pro-
ductive starting point for the discussion of the many types of autobiographical writings that surround what he calls the classical
autobiography: the memoir, the self-portrait, the letter, and the
diary. By distinguishing between grammatical person and "identity" we can deal more easily, for example, with second- and third-
person autobiographies (Lejeune, "Autobiography in the Third
Person").

One qualification that Lejeune himself makes to the question of
identity between author and diarist concerns the status of the
name of the author on the title page. As he states, "the place as-
signed to the name is highly significant: by social convention, it is
connected with the accepting of responsibility by a *real person* . . . a
person whose existence is legally verifiable, a matter of record"
("The Autobiographical Contract," p. 200). Lejeune is talking here
not in terms of any universal or ontological notion of selfhood but
in terms of a social contract particular to Western culture, such as
Michel Foucault outlined in "What Is an Author?" The emphasis is
on readers and texts, the proper name acting for the reader, as
Paul John Eakin puts it, as "the mediating term between the text
and the referential world that lies beyond it" ("Philippe Lejeune,"
p. 4).

To return then to the difference between *The Journals of Rayner
Heppenstall* as nonfiction and the *Diaries of Jane Somers* as fiction, we can say that Rayner Heppenstall is author, narrator, and
protagonist, and that his legal existence is guaranteed by the fact
that he (or now his estate) owns the copyright to the work, a legal-
ity recorded on the reverse of the title page.[1] Rayner Heppenstall
is, therefore, legally a real person who is capable of generating a
nonfiction diary; and not only the diary but, by implication, those
novels attributed to him on the flyleaf. This, according to Lejeune,
is important in autobiography since for the reader an image of the
autobiographer's world outside the text depends upon the writer
having produced other non-autobiographical texts: "the author is
defined as the person who is capable of producing this discourse"
("The Autobiographical Contract," p. 200). In the case of Rayner

Heppenstall, the diarist is writing from that "autobiographical space" (p. 216) that exists between his diary and his novels, and which gives the effect of a three-dimensional extra-textual reality.

The Diaries of Jane Somers is a combination of two novels which originally appeared separately. The first was issued as *The Diary of a Good Neighbour* and attributed on the title page to Jane Somers. The problem here in terms of Lejeune's identity relationship is that, as in the case of Heppenstall, the author's name is also that of the narrator/protagonist: "'My name is Janna Somers,' I said" (p. 39). Yet the work is still classified in Carmarthen Public Library as a work of fiction. We now know from the publication of the two novels as *The Diaries of Jane Somers* that Jane Somers is a pseudonym for Doris Lessing whose name appears on the title page of the compilation, and of pseudonyms Lejeune says: "A pseudonym is a name, which differs from that recognized by law, which a real person uses to *publish* some or all of his writings. The pseudonym is an *author's* name" ("The Autobiographical Contract," p. 200). In other words, a pseudonym is not exactly a fiction, it operates in the same way (or can do) as the author's real name—what is crucial is whether or not the narrator/protagonist shares the same name.

Unfortunately this does not help much in the present instance since Lejeune here is not dealing with cases in which the pseudonym is also the name of the narrator, and *The Diary of a Good Neighbour* attributed to Jane Somers still establishes the identity relationship between author and narrator necessary for autobiography. Here we have to introduce Lejeune's notion of *le pacte autobiographique*, sometimes translated as "the autobiographical contract" but preferred by Lejeune as "the autobiographical pact," connoting a less legalistic system of conventions rather than contractural rules ("bis," p. 421). The autobiographical pact is the actual means by which the text establishes how the work is to be read, the establishment of identity between the diarist and the author. Most often this is done *overtly* (Lejeune's term) by giving the diarist the same name as the author, though it may be done *implicitly* either in the title (*The Story of My Life*) or in an initial section "where the narrator makes commitments to the reader by behaving as if he was the author" ("The Autobiographical Contract," p. 203). It is a point worth noting that the autobiographical pact does not rely on a resemblance, on the level of events in the narrative between the diarist and presumed facts concerning the life of the author:

Even if there were all the reasons in the world for believing that the story was exactly the same, it would still be the case that the text in question was not an autobiography: autobiography supposes first of all that *identity* is assumed by the author on the level of the speech act ("énonciation") and, quite secondarily, that there is a *resemblance* on the level of utterance ("énoncé"). ("The Autobiographical Contract," p. 201)

We are now in a position to account for the fact that while *The Diary of a Good Neighbour* by Jane Somers establishes this autobiographical pact through the identity relationship between author and diarist, it is still categorized as a work of fiction. The account falls into two parts, both of which to some extent offer further qualifications to Lejeune's position. As we have seen, Lejeune himself makes the point that the autobiographical pact can be made in two ways: *overtly* by the establishment of identity between author and diarist in the course of the narrative and *implicitly* by the title or preamble to the work. However, in *The Diary of a Good Neighbour* these operate against each other, the publisher's blurb stating that the work be read as a novel—"*The Diary of a Good Neighbour* is a quite remarkable novel." This would have the effect of overriding the overt pact made in the text, especially as the blurb also tells us that the work is published pseudonymously—"Jane Somers is the pseudonym for a well-known woman journalist." Contrary then to Lejeune, here is a case where a pseudonym is indeed a fictional name, despite the fact that the pseudonym also operates as the author's name in the statement of copyright. If *Great Expectations* were published under the name of Philip Pirrip we might read it as autobiography, but if a preamble stated that it was a novel published pseudonymously by a well-known author we would read it as fiction. The crucial factor of identity in name between author and narrator/protagonist would be in this case no longer quite so crucial.

There is a secondary factor which may operate here and that is the question of the linguistic style and narrative structure of the work. Lejeune in "The Autobiographical Contract" is less interested in defining the autobiography by consideration of style and narrative structure than in analyzing the operation of the autobiographical pact. His only requirements of the text are that it be retrospective prose narrative: if the text is not retrospective it becomes a self-portrait or essay; if it is not prose then it is an autobiographical poem. However, while these generalizations may hold for the autobiography, both the nonfiction and fictive autobiography being written for publication, I think there is a discernible difference between the reader's expectations of diary fiction on the one hand and the nonfiction diary on the other, differences which relate to whether or not it is perceived from the style or narrative structure of the text that the work has been written for publication. Though such questions may not in most cases affect the classification of the works as fiction or nonfiction, any discussion of the diary and fiction must nevertheless also consider the text's style and structure. Certainly in the case of *The Diary of a Good Neighbour*, disregarding the overriding of the autobiographical pact, it would take a truly determined reader to read the work as nonfiction.

FICTION IN THE NONFICTION DIARY

In a collection of material drawn from the archives of the Mass-Observation Movement that began in Britain in the latter part of the 1930s, the editors make this comment about two diary entries (or Day Surveys) made by different Observers for 12 September 1937: "In contrast to the domestic immediacy of the first Day Survey, the second one has a self-consciousness and an air of composition which suggest it might be more fictional than actual" (Calder & Sheridan, *Speak for Yourself*, p. 6). This comment is in the same mode as those of Ponsonby and Spalding in the previous chapter, and it reveals again the cultural expectations of readers toward nonfiction diaries.

To begin with the first Day Survey, we can see that the editors are testing the authenticity of the diary against a need for the content to be "domestic" or, more generally, mundane. Evidence of this in the first Day Survey would be: "3.30 Clear away we wash up together. Children out in garden. I make scones for tea" (Calder & Sheridan, p. 7). This demand that the diary should record the mundane nature of everyday life is often matched by a demand that it be structured according to a mundane routine (breakfast, lunch, tea) or timetable (11.30, 2.15, 3.30)—the shape of the day is already given. Secondly, "immediacy" can be gauged by the closeness in space and time of the narrating voice to the events of the narrative, as in the place reference "Children *out* in garden" or the simple present tense "we wash up together." Deictic references such as these give the narrative a nonretrospective or intercalated viewpoint. And there is also the effect of immediacy in the style of the writing, the lack of punctuation in "Clear away we wash up to gether," the omission of modifying adjectives and determiners ("[The] Children out in [the] garden"), the omission of the copula ("Children [are] out in garden"), and the deletion of some pronouns ("[I/We] Clear away"). These are all features of a nonfiction diary style, as are others such as abbreviations and the use of logograms ("5 o/c") elsewhere in the entry, and the overall effect of these features is to make the work seem unliterary, unselfconscious, and written in a hurry. In short, the work is predominantly in what Geoffrey Leech calls an abbreviated mode, a disjunctive style which is distinct from the discursive grammar of literary discourse (*English in Advertising*).

In contrast, the second Day Survey has for the editors "an air of composition." Here there is still the concern for domestic detail, "When breakfast was finished I washed up while my brother fed the cats" (Calder & Sheridan, p. 11), and the events of the day are narrated in chronological order; but unlike the other Day Survey the syntax is predominantly more discursive, even though a few of the paragraphs do exhibit some of the features of the abbreviated mode ("Heard grandfather clock next door strike the hour, was sitting in armchair, legs up against the fireplace, book in my lap" [p. 9]). Moreover, the entry is both retrospective and written in a muddled range of styles from the colloquial ("I'd have been quids in this weekend" [p. 9]) and the idiosyncratic ("I was liking it better than any book I'd read for a long time" [p. 10]), through the relative complexities of interior monologue ("I'd wanted to hurt her for letting me down yesterday" [p. 15]), to the pseudo-literary ("Then in a desperate desire to hurt her I pulled the window down" [p. 9]). But what is most likely to have caused the editors to doubt the veracity of this account is the fact that, in contrast to the simple narrative structure of the first Day Survey, two episodes are developed across several paragraphs, the first a scene in which the narrator tries to hurt his girlfriend's feelings by not waving goodnight to her as she lies ill in bed in the house next door, the second a scene in which he goes to bed with another girl. Or almost goes to bed with her, for the account ends with the couple lingering outside the bedroom door:

"Let's wait another five minutes," I said. It was five minutes to twelve. She looked puzzled. "I'm an observer," I said. She asked me what I was talking about. I explained as best I could. "And today," I said, "is my very first day survey." She laughed. "But why wait," she said, "and lose what would probably be the best part of your report?" "There's a limit to everything," I said, pushing her in front of me as the clock next door chimed twelve. (p. 15)

This is the stuff of chapter endings, if not of the very best, and the use of narrative suspense coupled with a textual selfconsciousness indicates a degree of literary composition which sits uneasily with the work's status as a private diary.[2]

The point about these two Mass-Observation Day Surveys, then, is that as readers we evaluate their veracity or truthfulness by comparing their linguistic style and narrative structure. The more literary or discursive style pushes the second Day Survey toward fiction despite the autobiographical pact having been made in a preamble to both Day Surveys. Conversely, the more unlettered the style and the more fragmented the narrative, as in the first Day Survey, the more immediate it appears, the more we are prepared to accept it as truthful. We are thus dealing with two notions of fiction: although the diary is a nonfiction genre, it has within it the possibility of being fictionalized or fabricated.

To look a little closer at this question of veracity and what it implies, I have already shown how Lejeune does not place much emphasis on the veracity of the work of autobiography (the resemblance of the narrator to the author); Lejeune's stress is upon identity in name. This means that once the autobiographical pact has been made the work will remain an autobiography despite fears for its veracity. To be sure, Lejeune feels that the autobiography should resemble the truth "but it is not necessary that the result be an absolutely faithful resemblance" ("The Autobiographical Contract," p. 212). John Sturrock pushes this position to a logical extreme when he concludes of autobiography that "It is impossible . . . for an autobiographer not to be autobiographical" ("The New Model Autobiographer," p. 52).[3] I must say that I myself am in sympathy with this position, whimsical as it might seem stated like this, and if we suspect that the autobiographer is being economical with the truth then we assume this tells us something about the writer.

However, while we accept that an autobiography may be fictionalized and employ novelistic techniques, we are as readers less happy with the same tendency in the private diary. With autobiography we are reading a retrospective work in which the writer seeks to interpret past facts, or as John Sturrock puts it: "the writer is addressing us from the moment of writing, not from the moments he is remembering" (p. 56). Since the work is also written for a public, this reinforces a demand for dramatization. With the private diary, on the other hand, we look for a stronger underlying factual accuracy. Here, as in the Mass-Observation diaries, the stress is upon the events and observations of ordinary life. This, of course, does not and cannot preclude selection and interpretation but such interpretation will be both provisional and local since the understanding is that the individual entries are written close to the events recorded. Also, the need for a public and hence literary presentation will be less. In sum, if in the diary we believe we are peering through a crack in the curtains, in the autobiography the curtains are drawn back to present a stage.

The importance of this difference, though, is that it relies ultimately upon a comparison of linguistic style and narrative structure, and the effect of these on the reader. If the disjunctive or abbreviated style seems more immediate this does not necessarily guarantee either its composition or its factual accuracy. For the reader these are effects of style. In the two Mass-Observation diaries featured above, postscripts state that neither was composed on the day in question or from notes made on the day, and in fact the more literary, retrospective entry was written two days after the events it records, whereas the abbreviated, present-tense first Day Survey was written in two stages, seven and twelve days afterwards. This means that the first diarist had a clear knowledge of what constituted an appropriate diary style and that it is this style, not the conditions of the text's production, which gives the account what the editors referred to as its "domestic immediacy." The same point could be made about Pepys: as the editors there point out, although the diary went through a number of stages of composition and was written up sometimes three months and more after the events themselves, the abbreviated style shows that Pepys had a good understanding of what constituted an appropriate diary style (Matthews & Latham, *The Diary of Samual Pepys*, vol. 1: pp. cii–cv).

The point, though, is not the deterministic one that the adoption of a diary style fools some readers into reacting as though the diary were dashed off in the midst of the events it records, but that the diary style is always already a convention. Whatever the values accorded the diary by its many commentators (immediacy and authenticity, for example), the diary can never be an unmediated transcription of reality since it is constructed by written language and is a highly coded form of signification. Language cannot be neutral, transparent, or non-signifying, and in my approach I am, like Lejeune, stressing the cultural specificity of texts. For the reader, veracity and the difference between fiction and nonfiction is purely textual.

FICTION IN THE FICTIVE DIARY

In a negative sense, diary fiction is fictive because the autobiographical pact is not made—the diarist is not the author of the work but a character within it. This means that in most diary fiction the autobiographical pact within the novel, or rather its potential, is framed by a fictional pact with the reader. Where this frame is loosened, as in B. S. Johnson's *Trawl*, or shattered, as in Malcolm Lowry's "Through the Panama," there is a consequent unease and the text becomes a test of opposing readings, factual and fictive (see Chapter 7). Nevertheless, even where the fictional pact is made, the diary novel still has to decide how close to stick to the diary paradigm and, if it is to retain some of the cultural values attached to the nonfiction diary, it must adopt strategies so that it can depart from the paradigm and yet not overtly admit its status as a novel. What I will concentrate on here is the way in which diary fiction can depart from the diary norm without disrupting the cultural values invested in it. Later chapters can then concentrate on those areas where modern British diary fiction disrupts the diary paradigm in order to pose a more subversive challenge.

One convention of the diary is that the daily entries are written if not on the actual day then shortly afterward. This is associated with the demand for "immediacy" and "spontaneity," the diary as a record of the little incidents of everyday life. Thus the diary, though written retrospectively, is not retrospective in the sense of an autobiography and has not the same justification for the use of a discursive literary style. However, few diary novels slavishly record entries day after day, and, following a failure by the diarist to maintain regular accounts, the omission of several days, weeks, or even years allows the novelist both to vary the pace of the story and to use a more discursive novelistic style for the retrospective account of the events previously unrecorded. An associated technique involves an introductory summary of events so far or passages of autobiography inserted into the diary. The inclusion of retrospective, memoir narrative also allows the novelist to alter the order in which events are presented; the novelist can construct a plot from the chronological story for purposes such as suspense or thematic juxtaposition. It also permits the construction of chapters.

At the level of the story, the interruption of regular diary keeping can be naturalized by a range of excuses, the most common being illness:

Between my first entry in these pages, my first writing, and this dark page, many days have elapsed. Hell-hot days, days of raging fever. (Nye, *The Voyage of the Destiny*, p. 17)

As your lordship can see by the number at the head of this section I have not been as attentive to the journal as I could wish—nor is the reason such as I could wish! We have had bad weather again and the motion of the vessel augmented a colic which I trace to the late and unlamented *Bessie* [a cow]. (Golding, *Rites of Passage*, p. 62)

I've been ill.
    She's brought me a paper. The date says I've been here five days now, it feels longer. (Rogers, *The Ice Is Singing*, p. 53)

Once the lapse in diary keeping has been accounted for in this way, either through illness or overwork, the precedent has been established and further lapses may go unremarked. Such a divergence from regular diary keeping is noticeably more systematic in diary novels than in nonfiction diaries, but it is worth noting, as I pointed out with regard to Joe Orton's diary in the previous chapter, that in its surface form this is not restricted to fiction but is an imitation of a nonfiction technique. Moreover, by drawing attention to the lapse in diary keeping, such a technique is at once setting up a local convention of irregular entries while reinforcing the generic convention of regular diary keeping. In other words, here, as often elsewhere, by departing from a diary norm the text does not subvert the diary norm but actually endorses it.

Diary novels, like most novels, are also reluctant to specify the exact date of the entries—only the day of the month or the day of the week may be given, and there is often a reluctance to go even this far. As in the case of irregular diary keeping, the generic convention of dating is so strong that some reason is usually given for breaking it:

Another day. I have decided not to put dates as they break up the sense of a continuous meditation. (Murdoch, *The Sea, The Sea*, p. 26)

The year: you know it. The date? Surely what matters is that it is the first day of my passage to the other side of the world; in token whereof I have this moment inscribed the number "one" at the top of this page. (Golding, *Rites of Passage*, p. 3)

She laid the folded newspaper on the counter between us, and my eye
caught the words DISASTER, FAILURE and CRASH. It was also apparently a Tuesday, though date, month and year were concealed on the
other side of the fold. (Figes, *Nelly's Version*, p. 37)

This coyness about dating can be seen as part of a more general
tendency within the novel to distrust facts and to talk in terms of
truth as something deeper: "The inward man, the hidden face, not
just the usual surface resemblance . . . that is certainly my ambi-
tion here. But the style? My style? Is there indeed a style of the
individual voice? Or a more general style of truth to which individual voices aspire?" (Nye, p. 21). Whatever the reason for this
coyness about dating, there is therefore a double insistence when
dates are given ("this is factual" combined with "this is not really a
novel"), as in Robert Nye's account of Sir Walter Ralegh's last voyage, The *Voyage of the Destiny*, which is, if also more than, a historical work. The same is true of the public, political background
indicated by the exact dating in Doris Lessing's *The Golden Notebook* (the Red Notebook sections) and John Berger's *A Painter of
Our Time*.

Turning to linguistic style, few fictive diaries adhere to an abbreviated or disjunctive diary style. The most obvious reason for this is
that a diary in abbreviated style is difficult to read, the reader
having continually to supply a context by which to hypothesize
those elements of discursive grammar which have been omitted or
abbreviated. There are also other elements associated with the
abbreviated style that result from the private nature of the text,
such as a private or technical vocabulary, and many of these are
not recoverable by the reader. As a nonfiction example, I take a
passage from *The Diaries of Evelyn Waugh*: "Luncheon Buck's
Bridget and L. Herbert madly jaggering Howards cocktail party.
Saw Laura off to Clonboy. Cocktails Mrs Clifton. Dinner Travellers
Club: Billy, Chris, D'Arcy; jolly evening; drunk at the end (lie)" (p.
394).

In the nonfiction diary it is often the editor's task to explain ob-
scure terms in a footnote or in brackets (there are three editorial
footnotes to the Waugh entry) and such a device may be imitated in
the fictive diary, as in Robin Chapman's *The Duchess's Diary*. In
John Berger's *A Painter of Our Time*, where the diary has also been
translated into discursive English from its "original" Hungarian,
we can see how an interpolated commentary can allow the novelist
to imitate a text that requires of its reader a certain background

knowledge: "in order to complete the picture of these four years of a painter's life, it was necessary to have . . . a commentary of background facts" (p. 14). Of course, the footnote used in this way also functions to reinforce the notion that beyond the diary there is a real world to which the diary refers, a coherent public world of unproblematic facts. The fictive editor may also function to explain how the diary came to be published, again reinforcing the idea of the diary as a private text.

A more widespread excuse for the adoption of a fully discursive style in diary fiction is the acknowledgement by the diarist that the work may be written for publication, as in Lessing's *The Diaries of Jane Somers* ("Does that mean I really intend to publish this?" [p. 72]), or Iris Murdoch's *The Sea, The Sea* ("The reader, if there is one, may wonder . . ." [p. 18]). Golding's *Rites of Passage* draws on the letter-journal tradition by being written for a specific addressee, the diarist's godfather, and naturalizes the more public discursive style more openly. Nye's *The Voyage of the Destiny* is written for Ralegh's son Carew, and Miranda Grey in John Fowles's *The Collector* also feels the need to continually address someone, if only herself: "Minny, I'm not writing to you, I'm talking to myself" (p. 136). In general, it might be said that the use of the discursive style indicates a movement in the diary toward the more discursive forms of autobiography, such as the memoir, the self-portrait, or more especially the letter. Such strategies seek to account for the use of the discursive style rather than the more private disjunctive style of the diary without admitting that the work is a novel.

The difference between the narrative structure of the diary novel and that of the nonfiction diary is a little harder to demonstrate. As I mentioned earlier, the use of the diary form does not preclude passages of retrospection in which events are juxtaposed or inverted for narrative effect. It is also the case that often a novel will use diary sections for only local effect and so avoid the problems of the diary as a serial narrative. Let me start at the level of the individual entry. As we saw in the case of the first Mass-Observation Day Survey analyzed above, the personal diary has at its basic level a concern to account for the events of the day chronologically ("Got up. . . . Had breakfast. . . . Went shopping. . . ." etc.), with a consequent sequential paragraph structure where paragraphing is adopted. This is the diary recording the raw material of daily life (see Chapter 4). There are, however, diaries, often kept only for a short period, that relate to a particular series of events or a particular activity—wartime diaries, sea diaries, and artists' diaries are examples. Although daily entries may still be recorded, the emphasis is now upon a theme and such diaries provide more opportunity for discursive sections of interpretation or comment, however provisional. Fictive diaries tend to be selective in this way, enabling the author to develop the daily entries in a discursive style suited to more literary autobiographical forms. These daily entries offer both a complex structure of paragraphing by combining several themes, as well as an avoidance of disconnected events recorded chronologically:

A young man came to see me today. He claims to be my son. It would not, normally, have been an incident I would have thought worthy of recording in my notebook, but he was very persistent. I was engrossed at the time in my library book, and much struck by a passage in which the author describes human logic as a net of meridians and parallels thrown across the universe to make it captive. The more I thought about these lines, the more convinced I became that this insight had something to do with my own condition at present. I had escaped the net, just as, the author points out, the sun and stars had not conformed to the pattern established by man. A shadow came between me and the reading light in the quiet hotel lounge, falling on the pages of my library book.
    "Hello, mother," he said. (Figes, *Nelly's Version*, p. 118)

Here the arrival of the son frames the diarist's reflections on her reading, and both events are linked at the level of narrative theme or plot. The young man who presents himself as the diarist's son is soon to imprison the woman by a network of family responsibilities logically derived from his insistence that he is her son, "meridians thrown across her universe" to make her captive.

This discussion of theme in the nonfiction diary, the concentration of the diarist upon a linked series of events, leads on to a discussion of the narrative structure of the text as a whole. Unlike what we can expect of the nonfiction diary, diary novels have upon them the responsibility of the novel to give meaning to the series of daily events that have apparently occurred fortuitously. The expectation is that aspects of the diary will gradually combine to form a narrative structure or plot separate from the chronological series of events. That this is a convention of the novel rather than the diary is emphasized at the level of the story by the diarist pointedly discerning a pattern behind the daily diary keeping. For example, Robert Nye's Sir Walter Ralegh realizes his task is not merely to record his present voyage or even his past life: "Now the shapes come together, the shouts form a sort of a sentence. What sentence? 'The Voyage of the Destiny'" (p. 254). Typically this awareness of the diary as a self-contained structure coincides with a re-reading of the diary:

... we have come to an end, there is nothing more to be said. I mean—there is, of course, there is the daily record, but my journal, I found on looking back through it, had insensibly turned to the record of a drama—Colley's drama. *(Rites of Passage*, p. 264)

If I had time to keep this diary properly, it would have seemed a builder's yard, bits and odds stacked up, lying about, nothing in place, one thing not more important than another. You wander through ... and see a heap of sand there, a pile of glass here, some random steel girders, sacks of cement, crowbars. That is the point of a diary, the bits and pieces of events, all muddled together. But now I look back through the year and begin to know what was important. *(The Diaries of Jane Somers*, p. 145)

This last extract echoes Virginia Woolf's diary, the diary as capacious holdall into which "one flings a mass of odds and ends" in the hope that after a year or two "the collection had sorted itself and refined itself and coalesced" (*A Writer's Diary*, p. 23). It needs to be stressed however that such local passages have a larger function in the diary novel, naturalizing at the level of story a novelistic coherence quite unlike that of the diary. They also, yet again, reinforce the opposing generic convention of the diary, in this case as a formless transcription of empirical reality.

One final point remains to be made regarding the structural difference between our expectations of nonfiction diaries and diary fiction. If the perception of narrative coherence in the nonfiction diary, that "air of composition" noted in the second Mass-Observation diary, moves the work toward fiction, the reverse is not true of the diary novel. Diary fiction may achieve an effect of provisionality by disrupting any overall interpretation of the events recorded, as in Ann Quin's part-diary novel, *Passages*, where themes do not cohere in a systematic way and the story fragments into undifferentiated events; but this does not shift the work toward fact. In cases where a fictional pact with the reader has already been established, the work will be read as an avant-garde or experimental novel rather than as a strict imitation of the nonfiction diary. The same is true of style, where the use of a form of abbreviated style even for an effect of verisimilitude will not of itself be enough to question the status of the work as fiction.

THE RELATIVITY OF THE FORMAL DIFFERENCE
BETWEEN FACT AND FICTION

As I have been keen to stress, the difference between fact and fiction is itself a cultural difference, one that pertains at a particular time and in a particular society. As wider evidence of this we can cite the case of Japanese diaries written some thousand years ago.[4] Earlier diaries in Japan were written in Chinese, but the emergence in the tenth century of diaries in Japanese gave rise to a distinction between the private art diary written in Japanese and the natural public diary written in Chinese. However, the division of these two types into literary and nonliterary diaries is a modern one, imposed on the corpus since 1922 by Japanese scholars employing a Western esthetic notion of what constitutes literature. In the contemporary Japanese society, there was no concept of diary literature, and both types of diary were considered as relating to different aspects of the diarist. In our terms, the fictive diary and the nonfiction diary were both regarded as parts of our nonfiction diary.

The second aspect of the relativity of the difference between diary fiction and the nonfiction diary concerns the style and narrative structure of the two types. To take first the nonfiction diary, not all are written in an abbreviated style and the twentieth century has seen the emergence of a discursive diary which deals more with moods and emotions than with everyday events. As Robert Fothergill notes:

By 1930 Freud and Proust and Lawrence and Joyce—to name only these—had made it a formidable task to say who you are and what you did today. By 1930 the diary that really counts must express in the complexity of its organization and texture a creative response to this challenge. (*Private Chronicles*, p. 37)

It is interesting here to see that the argument is for a borrowing of the literary techniques of the novel, particularly the forms of stream-of-consciousness developed by modernism. Certainly such forms have been recommended as aids to a creative self-analysis.[5] Yet Fothergill goes on to argue that the great diarists creatively use the diary-format to produce a formally integrated serial autobiography, a "book of the self." The question here becomes one of deciding whether or not the wholesale borrowing of stylistic and structural techniques from the novel constitutes a nonfiction diary distinct from the fictive diary or whether it constitutes a movement toward fiction. To my mind, Fothergill's notion of the diary as on-going or serial autobiography rather than as a fragmented record of daily events has at its basis a desire to valorize selected diaries by reference to the memoir and hence ultimately in terms of a cul-turally specific tradition of great literature. Indeed, as I pointed out in Chapter 2, the corpus Fothergill chooses to survey is com-prised solely of published diaries and hence his examples have al-ready been through a process of literary selection. Such diaries do exist and are read as nonfiction, but they remain atypical and can-not be seen as constituting a fundamental change in the reader's notion of the diary as a genre.

So far as the fictive diary is concerned, as I have already men-tioned, not many works consistently use an abbreviated style. This style is most commonly limited to extracts of diaries contained in non-diary novels, as at the end of Joyce's *A Portrait of the Artist*:

20 March: Long talk with Cranly on the subject of my revolt. He had his grand manner on. I supple and suave. Attacked me on the score of love for one's mother. Tried to imagine his mother: cannot. Told me once, in a moment of thoughtlessness, his father was sixtyone when he was born. Can see him. Strong farmer type. Pepper and salt suit. Square feet. (p. 223)

Such extracts appear by contrast to the surrounding text less liter-ary and give an effect of immediacy. John Fowles has Miranda Grey in *The Collector* adopt an abbreviated style in illness: "(Morn-ing.) A really bad bronchial cold. Shivering. I haven't slept prop-erly. Horrid dreams. Weird, very vivid dream. G.P. was in one. It made me cry. I feel so frightened" (p. 266). Nevertheless, the diary novel does not exclude the abbreviated style, and shorter fiction can experimentally afford to risk reader failure by a predominant use of an abbreviated style, as in Malcolm Lowry's "Through the Panama" where the disjunctive effect reinforces strategies which cause the reader to doubt the fictional nature of the work: "*Dec. 11.* Gale still worse. Poor Salvadoreans and Dutchmen stuck in their cabins on after-deck: seas breaking right over: they can't get to salle-à-manger. Try to help but turns out couldn't matter less, they are all seasick" (p. 82). The same is true of Lowry's fragmented narrative structure where the hierarchical organization of the re-alist novel is questioned and the work progresses by the accumula-tion of disparate material:

A white dove comes on board.
And a jæger [skua] flies by.
And the French Government falls once more.
The little church bells that chime the hours. (p. 41)

If we now review the range of fictive and nonfiction diary writing, it is an impossible task to categorize aspects of style and structure according to whether they are to be found in fiction or nonfiction diaries. Both types have the potential to call upon all the resources of language. What we can do, however, as I have tried to do above, is to see style and structure in terms of their effect on the reader and to identify where a technique associated with fact or fiction crosses and occasionally recrosses the generic boundary. This is not to infer that there exists a specific example of a nonfiction diary which diary fiction imitates, not even within a specific culture at a specific time. No such model exists, firstly because, as I argued in Chapter 2, the realization of a paradigm occurs only in a changing historical context, and secondly because, as we can now see, what we are concerned with are features that are comparative, both internally and between texts. Who can say how regularly a diary should be kept or what the exact relationship should be between a simple paragraph structure and the use of the abbreviated style? Moreover, do such features have to be slavishly consistent throughout a text or can they vary in predictability? What we can say, however, is that an accumulation of novelistic techniques in the nonfiction diary or the lack of a theme in diary fiction can affect how the text is read, the nonfiction diary becoming suspect as a factual, private account, the diary novel departing from the traditional novel. Our reading of the text as fact or fiction depends in the end upon the particular configuration of the text we are reading and the way in which that configuration correlates with wider cultural values. The rest of this study will therefore be concerned with specific texts and the way in which modern British diary fiction rearranges diary features into configurations that not only challenge previous diary fiction but interrogate the discursive reality of a whole culture.

NOTES

1. For a discussion of copyright in the diary see my "Reading Other People's Diaries."

2. Both entries were of course written for someone other than the diarist, being sent to the Mass-Observation offices, but the distinction

still holds since we are talking here of comparative rather than absolute differences. For an interesting attempt at a typology of private diaries according to the position of the addressee see Jean Rousset, "Le Journal Intime."

3. Darrel Mansell, looking at autobiography from the standpoint of the author's intention, reaches a similar conclusion: "when we are determining which side of the great fact–fiction watershed a book belongs on, its conforming or not conforming to the facts of reality is irrelevant" ("Unsettling the Colonel's Hash," p. 122).

4. These remarks on Japanese diaries are derived from a combination of two sources, Bowring ("Japanese Diaries") and Miner (*Japanese Poetic Diaries*).

5. For the use of the stream-of-consciousness technique as "free intuitive writing" see Rainer, *The New Diary*, p. 62. The use of diary writing for self-analysis was popularized, systematized, and registered by the psychologist Ira Progoff. The diaries of Anaïs Nin are perhaps the most well-known of attempts at self-therapy through diary keeping.

4

Intertextual Writing:
The Diary as Raw Material

The commonsense notion that the diary records the raw material of everyday life is as pervasive and as hard to refute as the parallel idea that the holiday snapshot records what Auntie Dora really did to Uncle George on Brighton beach in 1935. Often the diary is itself likened to a snapshot: "The entry made on the day . . . is the snapshot, rough, unpremeditated—ill-composed and out of focus perhaps—but catching the fleeting expression which the carefully arranged and more finished studio photograph misses" (Ponsonby, *English Diaries*, p. 33). Of course, it is unlikely that the number of diaries brought back from a holiday comes anywhere near the number of films dropped in for developing, and the reception of the record—the snapshot onerously public, the diary inviolably private—suggests a greater personal investment in the diary. Nevertheless, both snapshot and diary can be brought out years later as records of times past, to aid or to correct reminiscence.

Such records, then, are held to be essentially factual, despite the technical limitations of the camera or the subjective interpretations of the diarist; the snapshot is displayed in support of an anecdote, the diary in support of the autobiography. In the case of a novelist's diary, the diary also becomes testament to the raw material from which the work of art is produced: "Katherine Mansfield's Journal shows her endlessly fascinated by those small, everyday incidents, humorous, pathetic or bizarre, which constitute the writer's raw material and the springboard for his imagination" (Willy, *Three Women Diarists*, p. 34). By the same count, it could be argued that the snapshots a painter may take provide a record of the raw material of his or her work of art. There is thus an implicit equation that fact plus imagination equals work of art. Leonard Woolf repeats this formula when he states that in his edition of Virginia Woolf's diary he has selected certain passages "because they give the reader an idea of the direct impact upon her mind of scenes and persons, i.e. the raw material of her art" (p. 8).

There are, however, problems with the notion of a diary as a record of raw material, and these correspond to an ambivalence in the notion of raw material itself. It is customary to think of raw material as a material that occurs naturally. Thus, iron ore is the raw material for steel production, wood the raw material for paper products, milk for dairy products, and so on. The idea of the diary as a record of raw material, therefore, has within it the notion that it merely records the actual, naturally occurring events that are the basis of the literary work of art. For example, Graham Greene kept a diary of his visit to the Belgian Congo when he was researching his novel *A Burnt-Out Case*. This diary was later published along with another of a wartime voyage to Sierra Leone, the setting for *The Heart of the Matter*. In an introduction to these diaries Greene writes:

Neither of these journals was kept for publication, but they may have some interest as an indication of the kind of raw material a novelist accumulates. He goes through life discarding more than he retains, but the points he notes are what he considers of creative interest at the moment of occurrence. (*In Search of a Character*, p. 9)

Greene is careful here not to accord the diary itself the status of raw material; rather, it merely indicates the nature of the material the novelist remembers. Nevertheless, earlier in his introduction he writes of his time in Sierra Leone:

I did not realize at the time that a novel would emerge from those years, and when five years later I began to write *The Heart of the Matter* I regretted my lack of notes. So many small details of life in Freetown had sunk for ever into the unconscious. I had stayed too long, so that I took too much for granted, for I have very little visual imagination and only a short memory. (p. 8)

The diary as a form of notetaking thus becomes itself the raw material of the novel: when writing his novel, Greene, with his short memory, refers back to the notes rather than the actual small details of life itself. In the case of Greene's trip to the Belgian Congo, the boat that takes Greene from the leprosery further up the river becomes, in *A Burnt-Out Case*, the boat that takes Querry to the leprosery:

A funny little high-built boat badly needing paint like a miniature Mississippi paddle-steamer. (*In Search of a Character*, pp. 35–36)

The boat, which was the property of the Bishop, resembled a small battered Mississippi paddle-steamer with a high nineteenth-century forestructure, the white paint badly in need of renewal. (*A Burnt-Out Case*, p. 9)

A close lexical comparison reveals that if we discount the two indefinite articles, of the eleven words of the first description five are repeated in the second description, five more are repeated either as synonyms or close forms, and only the word "funny" is not carried across, though its meaning is perhaps inferred in the term "nineteenth-century fore-structure." In other words, it is not the boat itself that is being transcribed into the novel but an intermediate description of the boat. It is a painting from a snapshot.

Now it is possible still to account for this in terms of raw material, as I have already hinted, by using a second meaning of the notion of raw material, that of a manufactured rather than a natural material used in the production of yet another product: paper is the raw material of books, steel is a raw material in the production of motor cars. Here the emphasis is not so much on the nature of the raw material but on the fact that one product is turned into a more sophisticated product. The diary is less sophisticated than the novel, the snapshot less sophisticated than the painting. The writer or painter takes the diary or snapshot and by a process of imagination turns it into a work of art.

A novel that uses this second notion more obviously than Greene is Robin Maugham's *The Last Encounter*. This novel purports to be the missing seventh diary kept by General Gordon while under siege in Khartoum, and, though it is less interesting in terms of the modern diary novel since it asks few questions of the form, it is interesting in the present context of the relationship between the nonfiction diary and the novel. While waiting for the relief expedition to arrive, General Gordon kept a number of diaries. These were sent down river to the approaching British forces, and six of these survived and were eventually published. They cover the period from 10 September to 14 December 1884. Maugham's novel covers the period 15 December 1884 to 25 January 1885, Gordon being killed when Khartoum fell on 26 January, and this fictive diary comes complete with a whole dossier of framing documentation explaining how the diary has only now come to light. However, a comparison of Maugham's novel and Gordon's published diaries shows that Gordon's record of the progress of the siege as related in the novel is in fact transcribed from the nonfiction diaries. In the novel, Maugham's Gordon records:

20 December
The Dervishes fired two shells at the Palace this morning. One shell burst in the air; the other fell in the river in direct line with the window I was sitting at.

   Three of my Arab soldiers deserted to the Dervishes today. But I discovered that these men had previously served with the Mahdi's forces and had now only returned to them. (p. 25)

This passage is compiled from extracts from three entries in Gordon's diary:

December 11
Two soldiers deserted to the Arabs to-day—these men are generally those who have been with the Arabs and had deserted to us.

December 12
The Arabs fired two shells at the Palace; one burst in the air, the other fell in the water in a direct line with the window I was sitting at, distant about a hundred yards.

December 14
Arabs fired two shells at the Palace this morning. (*General Gordon's Khartoum Journal*, pp. 218–19)

Such transcribed passages, it needs to be pointed out, do not provide the bulk of the novel; the novel is less concerned with the progress of the siege than with relating Gordon's sense of Christian destiny and his struggle to overcome a latent homosexuality. What is important is the way in which the nonfiction diary is transcribed into the novel without Maugham as transcriber having any firsthand knowledge of the events transcribed. In other words, what is transcribed is a discourse and not a personal experience, as could be argued in the case of Greene, where diary and novel appeared under the same author. Moreover, in the present case, this discourse remains a diary. The second meaning of the notion of raw material here prevails with Gordon's words recontextualized under Maugham's name.

We are thus moving into the situation where the diary is seen not to be dependent on what has happened in reality but, rather, exists as a separate form of signification. In terms of what I have called the raw material of the snapshot, Joel Snyder and Neil Walsh Allen have countered the notion that photography embodies "the manifest presence of authentic physical reality" by arguing instead that the way in which a photographic image is "characterized" and hence valued depends on such factors as the type of photographic equipment used and the position of the camera:

. . . "physical objects" do not have a single "image"—"their image"—but, rather, the camera can manipulate the reflected light to create an infinite number of images. An image is simply not a property which things naturally possess in addition to possessing size and weight. The image is a crafted, not a natural thing. ("Photography, Vision, and Representation," p. 151)

Snyder and Allen concede that something in the camera's field of vision will be represented in the image, but "how it will be represented is neither natural nor necessary" (p. 151). We can say, similarly, that representation in the diary is neither natural nor necessary. Moreover, to the degree that Snyder and Allen argue that the documentary value attached to an image is not inherent in what it represents but is in fact an interpretation, so we can draw attention to the fact that in Maugham's novel there is no linguistic distinction between what is fiction and what is nonfiction; the documentary value attached to a piece of writing depends on how it is read, and what can be read as nonfiction within the nonfiction diary can be read as fiction in a novel.

This failure of writing to record reality directly is a central issue in modern British diary writing. For example, one of the main concerns of Doris Lessing's *The Golden Notebook* is the different ways in which Anna Wulf transforms her own experiences into her novels: her experiences in wartime Africa become *Frontiers of War*, her five-year relationship with Michael becomes *The Shadow of the Third*, and her psychological breakdown is transposed into *Free Women*. But it becomes increasingly obvious to Anna that the non-

fiction or factual record of her experiences is not so untransformed
as she at first supposes. Having written an account of her experiences in Africa, Anna takes the usual commonsense raw material
view of her record: "That was the material that made *Frontiers of
War*" (*The Golden Notebook*, p. 162). Yet at a later date she notes: "I
read this over today, for the first time since I wrote it. It's full of
nostalgia, every word loaded with it, although at the time I wrote it
I thought I was being 'objective'" (p. 163). What Anna gradually
realizes as she keeps her diary is that form is not innocent and
that, whether she keeps a detailed account of her day or a brief
resumé, neither comes close to the experience of the day:

I am increasingly afflicted by vertigo where words mean nothing. Words
mean nothing. They have become, when I think, not the form into which
experience is shaped, but a series of meaningless sounds, like nursery
talk, and away to one side of experience. Or like the sound track of a film
that has slipped its connection with the film. (p. 462)

What has slipped here is the connection between writing and reality, and it is only after Anna has undergone a complete intellectual
breakdown in the climax of *The Golden Notebook* and passed beyond language that she is able to write about her experiences in the
novella *Free Women*. However, this is not an indication that the
connection between writing and reality has been reestablished; it
is rather an acceptance of the limitations of language to represent
what is real. Whereas Anna rejects both her previous novels for
their inaccuracy, her acceptance of the limitations surrounding the
portrayal of her experience of breakdown in *Free Women* reflects
Anna's wider acceptance of the limits of freedom.

    I do not wish to suggest that the argument of *The Golden Note-
book* is the one I am adopting here, particularly the metaphysical
argument that the truth of experience lies only beyond language.
What is interesting about *The Golden Notebook* in the present
context is its questioning of the notion of a diary as a simple transcription of reality and its demonstration that the constraints of
language operating in the novel affect all types of discourse. Language is not a transparent medium, and the relationship of the
diary to the novel is an intertextual relationship between two
highly coded forms of signification, two different types of discourse.
Both the diary and the snapshot appear less finished, yet there is
nothing about an abbreviated grammar or a grainy photographic
print which guarantees diary and snapshot as unmediated tran-

scriptions of reality. The assumption that the prior text is necessarily more directly connected with the raw material of everyday
life or reality, an assumption made particularly when the prior text
is a diary, is merely the result of the culturally specific distinction
between life and art being imposed on a relationship between texts.
Indeed, the whole notion of raw material itself, as I have tried to
demonstrate above, is one that depends not on the nature of the
material but on the relationship between products; a raw material
is only the raw material of something else and has no inherent
rawness; one person's raw material is another person's finished
product. The instability of this intertextual relationship is well
demonstrated in the work of Rayner Heppenstall.

In Rayner Heppenstall's novel *The Pier*, a mysterious first-person
narrator climbs onto a pier from a fishing boat in the early hours of
the morning and makes his way through deserted streets to his
own house. He remains there unseen all day, reading his desk
diaries for the previous four years, until at 4.40 pm he goes next
door and shoots his neighbours. He then walks back to the pier,
climbs onto the waiting fishing boat, and returns to France and an
arranged alibi.

The Pier is not, in its surface form, a diary novel; rather, like
B. S. Johnson's *Trawl*, it is a quasi-diary, that is, it is a periodic
first-person present-tense narration (see Chapter 7). The narrator
thinks rather than writes: "I am now on the upper deck of the pier,
by the ladies' and gents' conveniences, the buffet and the bar,
which will not be open for another four hours" (p. 7); "exceptions
may be found to my thought of a moment ago" (p. 160). Nevertheless, as is often the case in diary fiction, documents are recorded, a
newspaper cutting (p. 154), a brochure on the care of dentures (p.
157), and an entry from his desk diary for 31 August 1978 (p. 144).
Moreover, the narrator is conscious that he is narrating a story:
"The Metropole hotel will not enter much into my story, except as a
point of topographical reference. As that, it seems likely to assume
a certain importance" (pp. 21–22). The novel, therefore, has an am-
biguous relationship to written narrative.

This ambiguity adds a structurally complex dimension when the
comparatively straightforward chronological present-tense narration is related to the rereading of the desk diaries. Indeed, the
events of the day in question, 10 September 1979, form only about a
fifth of the novel's length. My interest in the novel is primarily in

the questions it asks of the relationship between novel and diary, and I will take this relationship in two parts, the novel in the diary and the diary in the novel.

In terms of the novel in the diary, the narrator who is later named as Harold Atha is himself a novelist. The narrator begins his rereading of his desk diaries with his purchase of his current house four and a half years previously in 1975. In May of the following year, the empty house next door is occupied by a large family of three generations, an event which is eventually to lead to multiple murder. Shortly after the arrival of these new neighbours, Atha begins his research into a new novel:

My reason for wanting to walk along the pier was to see the town from the end of it and to make a few mental notes of what I could distinguish. This was connected with a notion I had for a novel, which was to begin with a man walking in the morning from the end of the pier towards the town and to conclude with him in the evening returning to the end of the pier, with what intention I had not yet decided, might indeed never decide or at least never state. It might be suicide. (pp. 77–78)

However, work on the novel is disrupted by noise from the new neighbours, either from the children playing in the garden or from the building work carried out by the two men in the household, Fagg and Porringer: "We had had every reason to expect that the house next door would be bought by a quiet couple. . . . Now we were sandwiched, in a narrow converted coach house, between Clarendon Road and seven active people, with another on the way" (p. 67). And after a year of disturbance, his worsening relationship with his neighbours finds its way into Atha's novel, providing the motive for the protagonist to arrive at the pier in early morning:

A notion which recommended itself to me was that he should go home and get rid of hated neighbours and that his arrival and departure should be such as to constitute an unbreakable alibi for the inevitable murders, to which I could think of no credible alternative. In effect, the man would be myself, the neighbours Faggs, Porringers and Lamberts.

Writing a novel of which that should be the plot would not get rid of them, but it would afford me a fantasy satisfaction. (p. 137)

By the end of September 1978, however, an argument over a builder's ladder moves Atha to consider more than fantasy satisfaction: "This, I think, was the moment at which I first began to think of the plot of my novel as a possible scenario for action" (p. 154).

Atha's research into weaponry becomes research not for a novel but for the actual murders that take place at the end of *The Pier*.

The Pier, then, traces the formation of the plot for a novel in the mind of Harold Atha, a plot that Atha eventually uses as a scenario for personal vengeance. As such it is a good example of what Valerie Raoul terms *récit* becoming *discours*, "a story disguised as commentary" (*The French Fictional Journal*, p. 68). In other words, the reader first comes to the text with the awareness that it is a novel with a prearranged narrative structure (*récit*) and is then drawn into the seeming contingency of the events. On the other hand, the existence of writing as a subject of the novel means that it also works in the opposite direction, the seeming commentary or *discours* of the diary in the novel emerging as a story or narrative structure: the narrator "perceives his own *discours* in the process of becoming *récit*" (p. 68). In the present case, Atha observes the formulation of a novelistic plot.

Yet, as Raoul observes, this double reversal brings us back to the novel framing the diary, and in *The Pier* we become aware that the novel Atha first plans as a novel and then carries out is in fact the novel we have just been reading. This is where the ambiguity of Atha's narrative to written discourse is functional. Atha researches the opening of his novel (which is never given a working title) by going for a walk with his sister to measure the distance of his house from the pier:

At a hundred paces, I was by the engine for a boat called the *Maple Leaf*. At two hundred, I was just short of a bigger boat called the *Lady Haig*, which was still sticking across the concrete and had to be walked round. Three hundred brought us to the *Beau Jesse*, just short of a glass-fronted council notice board, exhibiting scanty notices of public entertainments. At four hundred paces was the winch for the *Good Turn*, and we were opposite the Sun in Splendour. At five hundred was the *Four Brothers*, and across the road was the Admiral Benbow hotel. At six hundred paces, we were already on the horseshoe ramp before the pier entrance. (p. 121)

This factual information is pre-echoed at the beginning of the narrative in the present-tense description of Atha making his way home on the day of the murders:

At a hundred paces, I pass the *4 Brothers* . . . at two hundred the *Good Times*, sitting pretty opposite the Sun in Splendour, the town's oldest public house, now much modernised. At three hundred paces come the

Beau Jesse and the notice-board which advertises piano recitals and
dances at the Pavilion.

An unusually big boat, the *Lady Haig*, for long stood across the espla-
nade at four hundred paces, the *Maple Leaf* undisturbed at five hundred.
(p. 10)

The description is, of course, in the reverse order and interestingly
the *Good Turn* becomes the *Good Times*, but such parallel passages
work both to reinforce the realism of the novel, its factuality, as
well as undercut the realism by making readers aware that they
are reading a novel that has the same form, if not in all cases
the same detail, as Atha's projected novel. Paradoxically, the novel
that emerges from inside *The Pier* is *The Pier* itself.

What, then, of the notion of the diary as raw material? In terms of
Harold Atha's research into his unwritten novel, the diary as a form
of note-taking operates in much the same way as we saw in Graham
Greene. We read the second description of Atha's "note-taking ex-
cursion to and along the pier" (p. 120) as the raw material for a
projected novel. It operates at a different level of reality to the novel
in the novel, giving factual authenticity to the fiction. On the other
hand, as we also saw in Greene, the high degree of linguistic similarity between a diary note and a passage in a novel means that we can
also see the note itself as raw material, as already a type of discourse
rather than a transcription of reality. And as sections of General
Gordon's diary can be inserted into a novel to be read as fiction, so
Atha's description of the boats on the sea front can operate both as a
factual note and as part of the introduction to a novel. The relativity
of the diary in the novel and the novel in the diary depend, as Raoul
rightly points out, on levels of discourse rather than on any essential relationship of one type of writing, the diary, to reality.

All that I have written so far might be seen as special pleading,
insofar as I have been talking mainly in terms of the position of
the diary in the novel. Although Raoul herself points out that the
movement from novel to diary precedes the movement from diary
to novel and so on *ad infinitum* (p. 76), she still privileges the novel
by the very fact that her study is a study of diary novels. It is
somewhat easier to deal with the relativity of the diary as raw
material in terms of metafictional works that are novels about novels, or more exactly, diary novels about novels and diaries. However, in the case of Heppenstall's *The Pier* we are in the rare
position of having in a published form Heppenstall's own diary

which covers the same period of Harold Atha's trials and tribulations with his neighbours.

The commonsense or empiricist view of Heppenstall's diary, as stated by Margaret Willy and Leonard Woolf, would be that this factual diary records the objective raw material that is transformed by the imagination into the novel as work of art. Heppenstall's diary concurs with most of the facts of *The Pier*. Heppenstall takes possession of Coach Cottage, Deal, on the same day as Harold Atha moved into his converted coach house, 19 July 1975. The layout of house and garden are exactly the same, and, indeed, the relation of the house to the pier is also the same. Both Heppenstall and Atha share a sixty-fourth birthday a week after moving house on Sunday 27 July. Both have neighbours move in next door a year later, and both suffer from the noise of the children and the building work. Indeed, a close comparison of diary and novel shows a surprising degree of agreement on almost everything recorded.

Of course, there is in *The Pier* a certain minimum degree of disguising, Heppenstall becoming Atha, his wife Margaret becoming Atha's sister Alison, Gilford Road becoming Clarendon Road, and so on. There is also much in the diary that does not appear in the novel, the result, we might argue, of the selecting and structuring of the raw material into an artistic unity. Now and again, however, detail slips into the novel without being disguised, the dentist called Bone who becomes Porteous in the novel, yet is once also referred to in the novel as Bone (p. 149); and it may be that the difference in the name of the boats noted above between the *Good Times* and the *Good Turn* is a similar instance. There is also a disparity of dating of the arrival of the Fun Fair in town, the end of September in the novel (p. 110) but the end of August in the diary (p. 223), due perhaps to a misreading of his own diary by Heppenstall. What is clear, however, is that in writing *The Pier* the situation of Atha sitting reading his diaries reflects Heppenstall reading his own diaries.

But there are certain complications to this commonsense view of Heppenstall's diaries. Let us start with another instance of parallel passages, this time not internal to the novel but from diary to novel as in Greene. In the diary, Heppenstall lights a bonfire and his neighbour calls the police:

Only a few minutes later, the doorbell rang again. It was a policeman, rather young, thin, dark, immaculate, quiet-mannered. He enquired whether I had a bonfire. I said yes and invited him in. He took his cap off, but would not sit down.

The course of that conversation I cannot quite clearly recapture. It ended in perfect happiness and even with jokes, and before that the young policeman had told us about the trouble his own wife had with a neighbour who lit bonfires every day when she hung up her washing. (*The Master Eccentric*, p. 193)

In the *The Pier* this is transposed to Atha's visit by a policeman:

Improbable as it may seem, it cannot have been more than a matter of minutes later when the doorbell rang again. It was a policeman, rather young and personable, thin, dark, immaculate, quiet-mannered. He enquired whether I had a bonfire and also whether I had been having words with Mr Edward Fagg (so that really was his name). I said yes on both counts and invited the policeman in. He took his cap off, but would not sit down.

The course of that conversation I cannot quite so clearly recapture. . . .

Thereafter the conversation became more general, if that were possible. The policeman told us about the trouble his own wife had with a neighbour who lit bonfires every day when she hung out her washing. (pp. 73–74)

These are clearly the same episode, and if we were to call *The Pier* an autobiographical novel, as it is tempting to do, we would have to point to the framing device of a man returned secretly from France to murder his neighbours as the element that turns the diary into a novel (we can assume that Heppenstall did not murder his neighbours, though the preoccupation with murder is also present throughout his diaries and is not of itself the novelistic element). This would seem to be how Heppenstall saw it, judging from the diary:

My reason for wanting to walk along the pier was to see the town from the end of it and to make mental notes of what I could see. This was connected with an idea I had for a novel, which was to begin with a man walking in the morning from the end of the pier towards the town and to end with him in the evening returning to the end of the pier, with what intention I had not yet decided. (*The Master Eccentric*, p. 198)

We should, therefore, be able to say that the Heppenstall diaries plus the frame of a man arriving at and departing from the pier becomes the novel *The Pier*, even if, as may be apparent, the novel itself contains the above passage from the diary and thus also the story of its own genesis.

But if the reading of the diary has an effect on the reading of the novel such that we must now call it an autobiographical novel, the reading of the novel has a reciprocal or dialectical effect on the diaries. To consider further the episode of the policeman's visit, in *The Pier* this episode is related by the narrator who is ostensibly leafing through his desk diaries while waiting for the right moment to commit the murders. The account of the visit is, therefore, written in a discursive grammar, appropriate to a novel, and narrated retrospectively, appropriate to the time of narration, complete with "I cannot quite so clearly recapture." And the bonfire in question concludes a narrative sequence that recounts the picking of quinces over a period of a week followed by the pruning of the tree and the subsequent bonfire.

In the diary, the picking of fruit and the bonfire occur on the same day. Something might be due here to the editing of the diaries for publication but this does not explain why the account of the policeman's visit in the diary is both discursive and retrospective ("I cannot quite clearly recapture"), features that allow large sections of the diary to be transcribed into the novel with little change. On the other hand, the diary entry for that day actually begins in the abbreviated style associated with diary writing: "Picked rather more than fifty quinces. The rest will be very difficult, if not impossible, to get at. Almost all are split, a consequence no doubt of the drought. Helped M., minimally, with the cutting up, which I found hard work" (p. 192). This can be contrasted with the novel version: "On Monday, with my sister standing beside the stepladder holding on to my trousers, I picked fifty quinces, but then did not feel that I could reach any more" (p. 71). The point, then, is that Heppenstall's diary itself is written in two distinct styles, an abbreviated, diary style and a retrospective, discursive style, and indeed once the reader is aware of *The Pier*, the large discursive sections of the diary read like the novel.

The reason for this is that Heppenstall kept two diaries. The first set of diaries are those bound desk diaries that Harold Atha in *The Pier* is reading. The second set of diaries are those that Heppenstall typed up periodically, mostly on Sundays but occasionally some months later, transcribing entries from the desk diary as well as working up events into a discursive and retrospective style. Following a slight stroke, Heppenstall notes in the published diary:

What is more immediately relevant is that I could hardly type. That is the reason why this diary contains no proper entries after July 2nd and why everything that I want to note for a month from July 8th has to be noted retrospectively. In my desk diary, I continued to make legible scribbles with great care, but I also have to tax my memory, which was unimpaired. (*The Master Eccentric*, p. 184)

It is these typed diaries that form the narrative sections of *The Pier*, the events related as though in Atha's mind. We are thus in the position of saying that not only do sections of the published diary read like the novel, their relation to the desk diaries is the same as that of the novel to themselves. Some sections of the desk diaries are both transcribed directly and transposed stylistically into the typed diaries; some sections of the typed diaries are also directly and indirectly transposed into the novel. Both diaries are raw material, the written diaries being the raw material of the diary that became the raw material that went into the novel. Conversely, if the novel is fiction by virtue of it being a rewriting of a factual discourse, so too is the typed diary.

Our search for the unadulterated raw material of *The Pier* would make it necessary here to go in search of the desk diaries, even assuming they have survived: Heppenstall destroyed all his diaries prior to 1969, as his diary relates (pp. 53–54), and there are no entries in the typed diary for 1979, the year in which Atha kills his neighbours and in which *The Pier* was written ("The nuisance from neighbours in part accounts for my failure to keep up this journal for over a year" [p. 243]). But enough has been said, I hope, to indicate that the result of such a search is likely to be unproductive. If we can say that the published diaries are not wholly factual because they are retrospective, then it is clear that the desk diaries, even if written on the same day as the events they record, will be to some extent retrospective, to some extent misremembered. And if the typed diary is not the raw material because it was composed from other documents, we will be forever searching for newspapers quoted from and letters received. This is not to say that the biographical project is invalid, only that as a project it can guarantee nothing about the diary as raw material. The status of the diary depends on a dialectical relationship between types of discourse, and it is this intertextual dialectic that is internalized in the diary novel.

To summarize the dialectical relationship between the diary and other types of discourse, let me return to Valerie Raoul's model of

the interaction between the structured story or *récit* and the un-
structured commentary on events as they occur, the *discours*. We
come to *The Pier* as a novel, certain aspects of the work such as the
title or blurb setting up expectations appropriate to a novel, a finished product or *récit*. The mode of narration, however, is that of
the quasi-diary, a nonretrospective periodic narration of the day in
question when Atha returns to murder his neighbours. Here we
are dealing with *discours*, the diary as raw material and the commentary on events as they occur. However, as Atha rereads his
diaries, it becomes apparent that the contingent events of these
diaries have themselves become a *récit* or story, a change of mode
reinforced by Atha's realization that they can form the basis of a
novel. As Raoul puts it: "As the narrator sees his life becoming a
book, his role shifts from author–narrator and character–actor to
that of reader–narratee: he perceives his own *discours* in the process of becoming *récit*" (*The French Fictional Journal*, p. 68).

The Pier is what Raoul would consider a variant of her model, in
that the rereading of the diaries is carried on in a separate narration from that of the diaries themselves. Moreover, the plot that
emerges from the diaries is not merely perceived as a retrospective
structure but one that Atha takes up and lives out; the *récit* circles
back into *discours* once more. Indeed, it is this movement, what the
blurb refers to as turning fiction into fact, that when set beside the
opposite movement makes *The Pier* so unsettling. The diary becomes both the book we are reading and the plot of a murder Atha
carries out.

Raoul's remarks on the nonfiction diary are perhaps less interesting, viewing the diary as predominantly a form of *discours* or personal narcissism. Raoul seems to accept the diary as raw material.
On the other hand, Raoul concedes that "as the narrator writes
about himself he tends progressively (more or less consciously) to
see himself-as-actor as a 'he,' and to perceive the contingent incidents of his daily life, as they recede into the past, as a story or
récit" (p. 11). It is this process that is internalized in the diary novel.
It seems to me, however, that while for the purposes of analysis we
can accept that "The diarist, while the diary is in progress, is
always relatively in a dialogue situation" (p. 11), once the diarist
puts pen to paper then the result is immediately a potential *récit*. It
is not, as Raoul suggests, the result of the passing of a certain
length of time or the diary reaching a certain number of pages: "The
narration, which functions as *discours* at the time of writing,
emerges as *récit* as the diary becomes a book" (p. 11). The potential

for the diary as writing to become *récit* may be realized immediately and after only one sentence has been written. This realization occurs, as Raoul rightly points out, when the diarist adopts the reader's position, but this shift is potentially immediate. In the case of Heppenstall typing up his desk diary at the end of the week, it occurs often the following day.

The position I am arguing, therefore, is that while at the time of writing the diarist may view the diary as a transcription of raw material or *discours*, as an object that exists as writing, as text, the diary is already a finished product or *récit*. *The Pier* then actualizes the potential of the nonfiction diary to become *récit*, and Heppenstall stands to the same material both as diarist and novelist. In Raoul's model, the existence of another text outside the diary novel which contains the same material but is directly in the novelist's name rather than the name of the fictive diarist gives to the diary novel as *récit* an additional frame as *discours*: "What formed part of a *récit* in the novel is brought back onto the plane of *discours*, but as commentary on life rather than on the novel" (p. 89). The diary in the novel is resurrected as raw material, and the dialectical relationship between *discours* and *récit* works across texts. Yet, as I have already argued, the diary is only seen as raw material when compared with a *récit*, be it an autobiography or a novel. There is no inherent rawness in the diary, and a novel might equally be seen as the raw material of another text. Moreover, when compared with a prior diary, the diary too becomes a *récit*.

In the case of Heppenstall, then, we have a series of texts all of which are both raw material and finished product: the desk diaries, the typed diaries, the novel *The Pier*, the diaries of Harold Atha, and the projected novel by Atha. Indeed, the same passage, word for word, might appear in all of them. Ultimately, what modern British diary novels like *The Pier* and, to a certain extent, *The Golden Notebook* are questioning (and one waits for the publication of Doris Lessing's diaries) is the notion that one sort of writing is closer to reality than another. The diary and the novel may be contained by different types of reading contract, but such reading contracts are shown to be culturally relative, not absolute. In seeing reality as dependent on the relationship between discourses, such diary novels are putting into question the cultural values that privilege—as being closer to an empirical reality—one type of discourse, the diary, over another, the novel. Our notion of reality, like the diary as raw material, has become destabilized.

5

Writing as Evidence:
The Private Document and Public History

In Chapter 4, I looked at the commonsense notion that the diary transcribes the raw material of daily life before it is transformed by the creative imagination into a work of fiction. The argument there was that this notion of the diary's rawness depended not upon any privileged relationship between the diary and reality but upon the relationship between different types of discourse. To the degree that a modern work of diary fiction such as Rayner Heppenstall's *The Pier* refused to privilege one level of discourse over another, it demonstrated both internally and externally the instability of the notion of the diary as raw material.

A notion that persists alongside the diary as artistic raw material is the diary as historical raw material, as source material for historical research. The diary from this perspective is closely related to the chronicle, the testament to public events close to their occurrence. John Tosh argues in *The Pursuit of History* that the diary differs from the chronicle in that "Unlike the chronicler or annalist, the diarist is as much preoccupied with his own subjective response as with the external events which he has witnessed" (p. 39). Indeed, the following entry from a Mass-Observation diary for 4 September 1939 is a good example of this subjectivity:

News of the *Athenia* [torpedoed by a German submarine] has just come through, I hope to God the world leaves Britain and France and Poland to wipe Germany from the face of the earth, until we do we shall never have any peace.

Fancy Jacqueline deciding to run a temperature, can I take her down in the shelter should an air raid come? or do I have to stay in the house? (Calder & Sheridan, *Speak for Yourself*, p. 163)

The importance of such an entry lies in the diarist's attitude to the war in general and in the effect of the war on domestic life; it is first personal and then representative. Few would go to this document for information about the sinking of the *Athenia* or the fact that war had been declared the previous day.

Nevertheless, although the subjective response may be dominant, its subjectivity is itself dialectically dependent on the public fact of the war. This particular diary begins (as presumably did many others) on the day war was declared, even though it is evident that preparations for war have been going on for some time, and the war provides the diary with an agreed public framework that makes domestic affairs significant. As K. Eckhard Kuhn-Osius argues of the diaries of Luise Rinser who was imprisoned by the Nazis: "She thus [in publishing her diaries] places the individual events of her life into a larger context within which they are to acquire their meaning. Her diaries are meant to be of interest within this context which is one of public knowledge and historical movement" ("Making Loose Ends Meet," p. 172). The private diary here, as in the one quoted above, becomes something more than a private diary and develops into a "private chronicle," to appropriate Robert Fothergill's term. The private and the public are mixed in one discourse, and the diary becomes a private record of public history in the making.

Before looking at those modern British diary novels that employ this notion of the private chronicle of historical events, I want first to examine the status of historical fact in the diary. As has already been pointed out, the diary as historical raw material parallels the notion of the diary as artistic raw material, and to this extent the facticity of the diary is pertinent to both. Recent developments in the study of history have shifted focus from the study of facts to the study of the way in which history is written, the division usually being seen as a division between history and historiography. Historiography as a mode of organizing facts into a narrative then becomes open to the same types of analysis applied to fictional narrative.

Hayden White is perhaps the best known of these exponents of a rhetorical study of history writing. White argues that facts are made comprehensible by the way in which they are organized into a plot-structure. Thus "histories gain part of their explanatory effect by their success in making stories out of mere chronicles" ("The Historical Text," p. 46). It follows from this that the same events can be given a different significance depending on how they are related: "The same set of events can serve as components of a story that is tragic or comic, as the case may be, depending on the historian's choice of the plot-structure that he considers most appropriate for ordering events of that kind so as to make them into a comprehensible story" (p. 47). White goes on to argue that the choice of plot-structure is not immanent in the events themselves but exists in the literary culture of the historian: "Properly understood, histories ought never to be read as unambiguous signs of the events they report, but rather as symbolic structures, extended metaphors, that 'liken' the events reported in them to some form with which we have already become familiar in our literary culture" (p. 52). Making history is, therefore, a cultural activity that gives meaning to past events within the terms of a culture's range of literary modes. It is narrative as a mode of comprehension which bestows meaning on historical facts (see also Mink, "History and Fiction").

The problem with this position is not so much its shift of attention from historical fact to historical narrative but the consequent shift from history to fiction. White himself admits that the endowment of meaning to historical events is a fiction-making operation, yet he still insists that historical fact is unchanged: "the data that are to be analyzed are not significantly different in the different accounts" (p. 59). For White, historical data can still exist as the "mere chronicle" from which historical plots are constructed. However, as Paul A. Roth has pointed out, even the notion of a chronicle involves a certain amount of fiction-making description. Thus, the "Ideal Chronicle" of the raw events "never gets started because there are no ideal events to chronicle. . . . Without some description or other, there are no specific events; with an identifying description, we still do not know if the event is of the requisite sort—that is, not primarily of our making" ("Narrative Explanations," p. 8). The diary or chronicle, then, even though it may be situated close to the occurrence of historical events, cannot record without also being an interpretation, a fiction, a way of making sense of reality through writing.

The more extreme form of this objection is put forward by Louis Gossman:

The simplest of events, after all, is itself a story, the interpretation of which involves a larger story of which it is part, so that history could be envisaged as a complex pattern of stories each of which contains another complex pattern of stories, and so on without end. There seems to be no outside of stories, no point at which they stop being stories and abut on hard particles of "facts." ("History and Literature," p. 31)

Historical raw material here disappears in much the same way as artistic raw material did in the case of Heppenstall. Gossman does not deny that there are such things as historical texts, but he locates their status as history within a larger system of competing narratives: "The fact that a story is presented as consonant with other stories and verifiable in relation to them establishes it as history. The rule founds the historical world; it is not derived from it" (p. 31). Consonance and not facticity identifies history from fiction and for Gossman there is no external historical fact, only significations of facts inside texts we call history. This is especially obvious when we note that reference to historical space and time can occur equally in the novel:

Interestingly, many novelists, anxious to give an air of history to their fictions, accept the space and time of the historian and try to observe this rule wherever their narratives do impinge on those of the historian. Space and time, in other words, do not appear to be objective realities that found the historian's work and differentiate it from the imaginary writings of the novelists, but rather a particular space and time act as signals to the reader that a work is to be regarded as history. The specificity of the text, in short, is not established by something outside it but by its own system. (p. 30)

Historical fact, insofar as it is consistent with other texts, operates in the novel in the same way as it does in the historical text. William Golding's Napoleonic War in *Rites of Passage*, we might say, is historical because it is consistent with the texts of history; in turn, the texts of history are historical because they are consistent with each other, not because they reproduce a historical event. And the objection that some historical texts such as chronicles and other primary documents are more privileged than others is met by the insistence that these are regarded as historical evidence only within the sign system of historical narrative: "The historian's narrative is constructed not upon reality itself or upon transparent images of it, but on signifiers which the historian's own action transforms into signs" (Gossman, p. 32).

It should be obvious from my examination in the previous chapter of the diary as factual raw material that my own position is very much in sympathy with that outlined above; namely, that there is no objective "outside" of historical narrative to which the discourse of history can refer. With regard to the notion of historical raw material, Louis O. Mink sums up the position thus: "'Events' (or more precisely, descriptions of events) are not the raw material out of which narratives are constructed; rather an event is an abstraction from a narrative" ("Narrative Form," p. 147). History is not there in the past waiting to be written. Mink, however, like White, is cautious about abolishing the notion of historical fact altogether (witness his qualifying "descriptions of events") and holds that "There can be only past facts not yet described in a context of narrative form" (p. 147). Yet like Roth, one is bound to ask where one can find facts that exist outside a narrative. And, indeed, is (to use my example from Golding) the Napoleonic War an event or a fact? Mink suggests at one point that these facts belong to the chronicle: "while objectivity is conceivable for a cumulative *chronicle*, it cannot really be translated into terms of narrative history" (p. 143; Mink's italics). Admittedly Mink himself questions this, but it is the nearest he comes to locating facts outside a narrative form; certainly his notion of a chronicle lies outside his definition of a narrative, that is, a textual unity that has a beginning, middle, and end, and which coheres by means other than a mere accumulation of events:

The difficulty with the model of logical conjunction . . . is that it is not a model of narrative form at all. It is rather a model of *chronicle*. Logical conjunction serves well enough as a representation of the only ordering relation of chronicles, which is ". . . and then . . . and then . . . and then . . ." Narratives, however, contain indefinitely many ways of *combining* these relations. It is such combination that we mean when we speak of the coherence of a narrative, or lack of it. (p. 144)

Mink here is using the notion of logical conjunction to demonstrate the difficulties of assigning a truth-value to the more complex form of historical narrative. The difficulty in this for me is not only that it would be difficult to find a diary that progressed merely by logical conjunction or temporal succession, or indeed that each event or entry may be a narrative in Mink's own sense; the main difficulty is that I cannot see that logical conjunction is not also a mode of narrative. As E. M. Forster famously puts it: "'The king died and then the queen died,' is a story. 'The king died, and then the queen died of grief,' is a plot" (*Aspects of the Novel*, p. 93). Using Forster's typology we can say that a story may be less complex than a plot but it is a narrative nonetheless and certainly a war diary or chronicle would have a clear beginning, middle, and end. Yet Mink would certainly not claim that a war as a historical event was not abstracted from a narrative form: "An event may take five seconds or five months, but in either case whether it is one event or many depends not on a definition of 'event' but on a particular narrative construction which generates the text's appropriate description" (p. 147). I would also add that even a chronicle must have a narrator, however effaced such a figure may appear to be (a point that also makes Benveniste's distinction between *discours* and *histoire* problematic). Therefore, it is worth stressing once again that, where one is talking of the diary as a private chronicle or succession of events, one is still talking in terms of events or facts inside a narrative frame; a chronicle is not necessarily closer than narrative history to a nonnarrative historical fact.

Nevertheless, despite such difficulties about what actually might constitute a historical fact, Mink's comments with regard to a second distinction, that between history and fiction, would I think be generally accepted: "our understanding of fiction needs the contrast with history as much as our understanding of history needs the contrast with fiction. . . . If the distinction were to disappear, fiction and history would both collapse back into myth and be indistinguishable from it as from each other" (pp. 148–49). Here the textuality of history falls under the control of genre; our understanding of the difference between history and fiction is certainly institutionalized and it depends, I suggest, not on the facticity of history but on the very relationship between texts that Mink highlights. In a culture that has no such generic distinction, we do indeed collapse the two into myth. As in the case of the diary as the raw material of the novel, we are again talking in terms of intertextual relationships and a cultural hierarchy of discourses, the cultural validation of history as more factual than the novel. Historical narrative (and here I include the private chronicle) is now seen less as a recording of a fixed past and more in terms of the relativity of texts.

The efficacy of this relativizing or textualizing of history can be gauged by turning to a recent critical work which accepts that historical reality exists independent of its representation in writing.

In *Perspective in British Historical Fiction Today*, Neil McEwan, as his title suggests, works from "the traditional assumption that perspective is possible because the past is independent of our reconstructions of it" (p. 12). In other words, "Historical novelists are privileged by our consent in their freedom to speculate but they are constrained by the real, and they will not hold attention unless they respect the past which is common to all readers" (p. 13). McEwan is well aware of the kind of objections to his position I have outlined above and quotes from Roland Barthes's critique of the referential nature of history in "The Discourse of History" (a position exemplified by Gossman above). However, where Barthes is held to claim that both realism and historical narrative are dying out, McEwan argues that "The following chapters try to show that they are not, and that their union in historical fiction enriches our culture by protecting the past which in Barthes's theory falls away, like reality itself, leaving the dullness of solipsism to which all such reductionism tends" (p. 17).

It is hard to counter McEwan's argument without merely repeating the arguments above and of which McEwan is aware. Moreover, as Mink points out:

. . . that past actuality is an untold story is a presupposition, not a proposition which is often consciously asserted or argued. I do not know a single historian, or indeed anyone, who would subscribe to it as a consciously held belief; yet if I am right, it is implicitly presupposed as widely as it would be explicitly rejected. ("Narrative Form," p. 135)

McEwan comes close to claiming this presupposition as a proposition, and his motive seems to be a belief in traditional liberal values: "the traditional assumption that . . . the past is independent." His proposition is laced with such terms as *respect* for the past (*Perspective*, p. 13), the *integrity* of the past (p. 6), and "A sceptical but firm sense of *values*" as "a good basis for looking at the past" (p. 7; my italics). What McEwan is arguing against is "a fashionable kind of doctrinaire scepticism" (p. 13), and he prefers the writings of A. J. P. Taylor to those historians who have made "synchronic analysis more fashionable than narrative" (p. 17). In sum, McEwan is appropriating the idea of the independence of the past in order to reassert those traditional liberal values he feels are under threat from the intellectual fashions of modern society. Like Robert Fothergill, McEwan is claiming that his own ideology is natural, self-evident, and not an ideology at all.

McEwan's study, not surprisingly, therefore, praises the realism of both Mary Renault and J. G. Farrell; Anthony Burgess and Robert Nye (for *Falstaff*) are allowed in because they accept the way the past is encoded in the language of today. In a chapter on John Fowles and William Golding, Fowles fares not so well against Golding: "Fowles's *The French Lieutenant's Woman* (1969) is fashionably 'troubled' by theoretical questions of form and status in contemporary fiction; Golding's *Rites of Passage* (1980) is not troubled at all. . . . Golding's novel is a well-made work whose form is subject to the author's imagination and to nothing else" (p. 159). What McEwan fails to see is that *Rites of Passage* is in the form of a diary; or rather, he is unable to see the ideological nature of the assumptions the diary form carries with it, because they are congruent with his own ideological assumptions about an essential human nature: Golding's real purpose "assumes that one age is much like another, in the essentials" (p. 176). But by ignoring the technical strategy of Golding's novel, its discursive form, McEwan is inconsistent with his own position of granting integrity to the past. The diary that Edmund Talbot keeps is not the modern *journal intime* but an eighteenth-century letter journal; moreover, Golding's novel as a whole relies on the model of the late eighteenth-century letter-journal novel (see Chapter 7). This is not a question of Golding's imagination but of Golding's technical skill in reworking a fictional form appropriate to the period in which the story is set. *Rites of Passage* depends on an eighteenth-century narrative convention which is high in intrigue and low in introspection, a technique that builds up the character of Talbot as someone who believes, at least at the beginning of the novel, in what we would regard now as the superficial social forms of the time. It is only by a breaking down of these social forms (and in the course of the immediate sequel, *Close Quarters*, a breaking down of the form of the letter-journal novel) that introspection and a move toward a post-Romantic or nineteenth-century view of the individual as isolated from society can take place. It is not incidental that the novel is set at the end of the Napoleonic War since it is the ending of this war which leads to a radical realignment of the social order. The letter journal in *Rites of Passage* stands for the relativity or historical evolution of narrative form itself and its role in social change. Golding's novel charts the emergence of those cultural beliefs McEwan then reads back into the novel in an ahistorical way.

Louis O. Mink asserts the relativity of commonsense: "common sense of whatever age has presuppositions which derive not from universal human experience but from a shared conceptual framework, which determines what shall count as experience for its communicants" ("Narrative Form," p. 129). McEwan's pre-supposition about the independence of the past is based on the commonsense notion that history and fiction are different; but his appropriation of historical fiction to demonstrate an essential human nature which would counter the vagaries of contemporary fashion is ultimately self-defeating. The relativization of history does threaten a belief in an essential human nature, but it is only solipsistic if one holds that belief. In itself, the notion that history and fiction are different, not because of the facticity of history but because a specific culture discriminates between narrative texts for its own purposes, does not necessarily lead to cultural decadence. It is salutary precisely because it demonstrates that timeless values are themselves not timeless but culture specific. Moral relativity, especially in a multi-cultural society, is not the same as immorality.

It has to be admitted that those diary novels set in a remote historical period do not question the notion of history so radically as those that deal with the contemporary political situation, as in Doris Lessing's *The Golden Notebook* or John Berger's *A Painter of Our Time*. Robert Nye in *The Voyage of the Destiny* and Robin Maugham in *The Last Encounter* take historical characters (respectively Sir Walter Ralegh and General Gordon) and trace in their reconstructed diaries the unknown man behind the public legend. History in both cases is to a certain extent domesticated, brought down from high politics to the everyday, but this is done largely through an acceptance of the diary as evidence. History is questioned only in the way that the narrative event of, in these cases, Ralegh's last voyage or Gordon's besiegement in Khartoum is broken down into the chronicle of the events that comprise historical narrative. The everyday facticity of the diary cannot be questioned, because the conceit of these novels is that they give the historical raw material out of which the narrative legend is created. As private chronicles these diaries purport to be public and therefore accurate historical testament.

In Golding's *Rites of Passage* and especially in its immediate sequel, *Close Quarters*, the diary again has a public historical frame: the year 1815 and the ending of the Napoleonic wars. Here, however, the central character is not a historical figure, though he has a public post as assistant to the Governor of the English colony of

New South Wales. The novel is less a public testament aimed at correcting an inaccurate historical interpretation than an autobiographical confession; and the element of history is important not because of its inaccuracy but, on the contrary, precisely because it accurately highlights the individual against a historical background. If Nye and Maugham choose a diarist who understands his participation in history, Golding chooses a diarist who finds it hard to conceive of historical significance: "I tried once more to realize the fact—a turning point in history, one of the world's great occasions, we stood on a watershed and so on—but it was no use. My head became the arena of confused images and thoughts" (*Close Quarters*, p. 54). Whereas Ralegh and General Gordon have an eye on that future which will turn their present into history, Golding's Edmund Talbot cannot conceive of a future different from his present and so cannot come to terms with its historical significance. The relationship between accepted history as a fiction and the private diary as fact posited in Nye and Maugham is reversed, and the failure outlined in *Rites of Passage* lies not with history but in the foresight of the diarist: history here is correct.

History as ideological construct and historical perspective as open to negotiation is dealt with, then, not in historical diary fiction like Nye and Golding but in those diary novels that deal with contemporary history, a history for which at the time of the novel's composition there is as yet no widely accepted historical overview. My term "contemporary history" is something of an oxymoron, in that the notion of history assumes a certain time-lapse before events become historical, the time-lapse necessary for an accepted historical perspective to be established. The distinction I wish to make is between those modern works that situate the fictive diarist in a previous century and are thus easily perceived as historical novels, and those that situate the diarist in the period of the novel's composition. The historical aspect in these cases is the degree to which the novel deals with the political and social issues of its time, those issues which will serve to categorize the period at a later date. In short, the historical aspect is the public frame against which the diarist as a private individual writes.

For example, in Rayner Heppenstall's *The Pier*, the succession of personal details recorded by Harold Atha is gradually permeated by references to contemporary news, such as the picketing at Grunwick's in July 1977, the legal proceedings against Jeremy Thorpe which ended on 13 December 1978, and a whole catalogue of domestic events: "The trade-union war against hospital patients continued, and Christmas television was threatened. The IRA bombed Christmas shoppers and machine-gunned guardsmen. As Iranian oil dried up, a petrol strike seemed likely here. Hugh Scanlon was made a life peer on his retirement from striking" (p. 164). Three aspects of these references are important here. The first is that Atha has no personal experience of these events; they are, on the contrary, lifted from the news media: "These facts about life in the great outside world I discover from a pile of copies of the *Daily Mail* which has accumulated over a period of almost a year. . . . I may continue to refer to them in the time that remains" (p. 160). In other words, these events may be facts to the degree that they have appeared in a newspaper, but those public events recorded in *The Pier* are a selection. This leads to a second aspect, that the principle behind the selection of events reinforces the character of Atha, his interest in court proceedings being consistent with his work as a criminal historian, and the mounting chronicle of union strikes characterizing his own political position. Third, the chronicle presented of the time is one of failing political and social cohesion, the kind of failure represented by the breakdown of Atha's own relationship with his neighbours. In *The Pier*, the private side of the diary as private chronicle remains the strongest, yet the novel demonstrates how a selection of public events produces a chronicle that interacts with the private events of the diarist to produce a public narrative. Harold Atha is not only recording his private life but at the same time creating a right-wing contemporary history. History has become a fiction.

The collapse of the difference between history and fiction is a well-worn theme in American fiction, where the public events that comprise contemporary history tend toward the fantastic. A good instance of this in terms of diary fiction is Kurt Vonnegut's *Mother Night* in which an American who may not be an American is at once a Nazi war criminal and an American spy; his attempts to prove his innocence collapse when the facts of his wartime activities can be interpreted in opposing yet equally valid ways, leaving him unsure himself whether he is innocent or guilty. In British fiction, the facticity of history has proved more resilient, though the kind of questioning undertaken by American writers has still taken place. Malcolm Bradbury's *The History Man* is testament to the force of this threat, in its implications both for the liberal humanist concept of a free and self-governing individual, and for a belief in the objectivity of history, the lynchpins of the unified plot-structure of the

nineteenth-century realist British novel. As McEwan puts it from
his perspective: "the denial of perspective which follows from 'the
death of the past,' 'all history is contemporary history,' 'history has
no *mythic* authority,' leads to fantasy or to propaganda" (*Perspective*, p. 183).

From this point of view, it is perhaps possible to see Heppenstall's *The Pier* as a move into propaganda, a rather (and perhaps
in the end too obviously) one-sided view of contemporary history. It
is equally possible to see it as the fantasy of a jaundiced eccentric.
Doris Lessing's questioning of history in *The Golden Notebook* is,
however, less easily dismissed. In a more extreme move than
Harold Atha's, Lessing's Anna Wulf at one stage gives up writing
personal entries in her diary in favor of recording only public
events; moreover, her method of recording is actually to cut the
news items from the newspaper and paste them in. For example:
"July 13th, [19]50 There were cheers in Congress today when Mr
Lloyd Bentsen, Democrat, urged that President Truman should tell
the North Koreans to withdraw within a week or their towns would
be atom-bombed. [*Daily*] *Express*" (p. 242). The first point to notice
about such a strategy is its effect in destroying the distance between fiction and fact appropriate to the fictive status of the novel.
While it is possible to control one's response to the events contained
in *The Pier* because of the character of the narrator, here the inser-
tion of a seemingly actual and verifiable public document into a
private diary coupled with its continued contemporary relevance
pulls a work of fiction directly into the mode of public history. The
second effect is to create a chronicle that, though it traces the
progress of a limited number of topics such as the development of
the hydrogen bomb and the war in Korea, does not coalesce into a
narrative explanation. It is perhaps this effect, anathema to the
conventional realist novel, to which Mink draws attention when he
makes the distinction between chronicle and historical narrative.
The chronicle works against the totalization of events into a historical narrative and demonstrates the absurdity of contemporary
history: "22nd March, 1952 The charge that the United Nations are
using bacteriological warfare in Korea cannot be dismissed merely
because it would be insane. [*New*] *Statesman*" ("History and Fiction," p. 245). This absurdity is the same as is found in American
fiction where, as in Vonnegut, events exceed moral, ethical, or even
logical reasoning. Narrative coherence is disrupted by the contingency of events.

Anna Wulf's reason for temporarily abandoning the personal side of the private chronicle is partly to record what she sees as the underlying destructiveness of humanity: "what I've got is a record of war, murder, chaos, misery" (p. 251). The lack of order in the chronicle is thus a representation of the chaos of contemporary life ("the real movement of the world toward dark, hardening power" [p. 568]), the acceptance of which Anna Wulf must, as I argue in Chapter 8, work toward in order to overcome the disintegration of her personality. In terms of the novel itself, therefore, this apparent historical raw material is nevertheless meaningful in the same terms as I applied to *The Pier*: it is again a selection of events; this selection is personal and characterizes the chronicler (at the very least as a reader of the *New Statesman* and the *Daily Express*); and the destructiveness of public events mirrors the events in the diarist's private life. Again, historical events are not quite so objective as they are presented to be.

Yet public history is not quite so subjective as it appears in *The Pier*. The comparable American case that I have mentioned, Kurt Vonnegut's *Mother Night*, relies precisely on the tension being maintained between the public and the private; the absurdity depends on the reader accepting the facticity of the Second World War yet being willing to accept that the diarist's account, though seemingly fictitious, is equally factual. This is achieved partly because the novel mimics the nonfiction form of the diary; yet in the main this tension is achieved because the narrator himself is, unlike the narrator of *The Pier*, directly involved in the public events he relates. The position is similar in Lessing where Anna Wulf as an active member of the Communist Party has been involved directly in the progress of Communism in Great Britain, albeit less violently than her record of its progress in Korea, America, and Eastern Europe; in other words, the two areas of public and private overlap. The position is, of course, also the same in both Nye and Maugham, where Ralegh and General Gordon are commenting about their own historical roles. But the difference is that, where Ralegh and Gordon attempt to rectify an inaccurate future historical perspective (in the name of an objectively truer history), in Lessing the attempt is primarily to synthesize private fact with public fact. Anna Wulf's personal disintegration is a concomitant of the chaos of world events, and the two inhabit a common facticity. Her solution has finally to involve a transcendence of the division between subject and object:

"What do you think this thing is that makes people like us have to experience everything? We're driven by something to be as many different
things or people as possible." He heard this, and said: "I don't know. I
don't have to try, it's what I am." I said: "I'm not trying. I'm being driven.
Do you suppose that people who lived earlier were tormented by what
they had not experienced?" (pp. 590–91)

Anna Wulf is a woman of her time, and history resides neither in
personal experience nor in the public realms of the newspaper but
is negotiated in the space between the two.

All the novels so far mentioned examine the relationship between the private and the public, the twin poles of the notion of the
diary as private chronicle. Where they differ is that while Nye,
Maugham, and Golding privilege the one or the other as factual,
depending on whether or not they want to invest the diary with a
higher truth-value, Heppenstall and Lessing are unwilling to make
that commitment: in Heppenstall the public fact is as subjective as
the private response; and in Lessing, both history and the individual are finally synthesized in terms of what the novel sees as a
visionary overview that transcends the subject/object division involved in the distinction between private and public, fiction and
history. The cultural division between private and public narratives is called into question.

To develop this questioning of these interrelated dichotomies of
subject/object, private/public, fiction/history, I want finally to turn
to John Berger's diary novel, *A Painter of Our Time*. Like Lessing's
The Golden Notebook, Berger's novel is concerned with the political
events of the 1950s, and the political engagement of the central
character stems from his position as a Hungarian painter living in
exile in London just prior to the Hungarian revolution of October
and November 1956. The title itself, *A Painter of Our Time*, thus
refers explicitly to the conjunction of the private and the public,
the individuality of the artist in relation to world events.

The notion that someone is or is not of their time depends, as is
evident, on locating the individual in an intersubjective temporal
framework. This framework involves two timescales, clocktime and
the calendar. As Peter L. Berger and Thomas Luckmann put it in
The Social Construction of Reality:

The temporal structure of everyday life not only imposes prearranged
sequences upon the "agenda" of any single day but also imposes itself
upon my biography as a whole. Within the coordinates set by this tem-

poral structure I apprehend both daily "agenda" and overall biography. Clock and calendar ensure that, indeed, I am a "man of my time." Only within this temporal structure does everyday life retain for me its accent of reality. (p. 42)

Reality for Berger and Luckmann is, as their own title suggests, constructed socially and is a coercive element beyond the control of the individual: "The temporal structure of everyday life confronts me as a facticity with which I must reckon, that is, with which I must try to synchronize my own projects" (p. 41). In writing a diary one is thus invited by the form to locate oneself against both these timescales, that of the clock and that of the calendar.

It is important to remember, however, that the "facticity" to which Berger and Luckmann refer may appear to the individual as something fixed and ontologically essential because it resides outside the individual, but it is nonetheless a social construct: not all cultures keep to the same calendar, and the clocktimes themselves are flexible, witness the absurdist concept of double British Summer Time (moving clocks forward two hours from Greenwich Mean Time during the summer). Time, and indeed space, are relative to their context. As Gossman puts it with reference to history: "Space and time are not absolute but are themselves defined by the historian" ("History and Literature," p. 30). And when Berger and Luckmann state that the calendar "provides the historicity that determines my situation in the world of everyday life" (p. 41), it becomes clearer that public or historical time is something that is open to some negotiation between competing groups of society, groups that at the same time compete to define history. We return here to my criticism of McEwan.

We can say, therefore, that John Berger's title, *A Painter of Our Time*, although seemingly objectified against the events in Hungary of the 1950s, has a political significance in terms of the appropriation of a contemporary history from a specific cultural viewpoint. The novel itself enacts this appropriation in two ways. First, the diary of the painter, Janos Lavin, is presented to the reader through an editorial introduction which explains how the work came to be published. The experience of the painter is presented as a cultural exemplum, and the diary itself as personal testament is given the force of a public document, as evidence about the times in which it was written: "it amounted to a *Portrait of the Artist as an Emigré*, and today in one sense or another most artists are *émigrés*" (p. 14). Moreover, through an interpolated edi-

torial commentary, the events related are invested with a certain
significance under the guise of making them accessible to a public
readership. For example, after Lavin records making an etching,
the fictive editor comments: "He wipes the ink off the plate, and
between each wipe cleans his hand by rubbing it on the apron down
his thighs. . . . The smell, the harsh light, the intent physical patience of the man, suggest a basement cobbler. And there is something of the artisan in his pride" (p. 21). Here, the historic present
dramatizes the artist as worker, a correlative of the paintings
Janos himself makes of the welder: "NOVEMBER 26. Have begun
a canvas of a welder. I watch him in the workshop round the cor-
ner. Despite gloves and mask, his action must have the precision of
a Renaissance Cupid touching Venus's tit" (p. 160). In the twentieth century, "in our time," the artist is a worker, the worker an
artist.

The second way in which *A Painter of Our Time* enacts the appropriation or, to put it less contentiously, the creation of historical
perspective, is the way in which the diary portrays the growing
involvement of Lavin in contemporary events. From being an unknown and solitary artist working in a studio in London and
prompted by the political execution in Hungary of his friend Laszlo,
Lavin gradually comes to recognize the necessity of his return to
Hungary: "I have chosen to spend my life on my art, instead of on
immediate objectives" (p. 76). As in Lessing, then, the diarist is
directly involved in world events and, again as in Lessing, finally
rejects the opposition between private and public that is sustained
in Nye and Maugham. Although Lavin abandons his artistic life in
London, he does so at a time when, with growing recognition of his
work in critical circles, he finds his political commitment being
appropriated by effete gallery owners and rich collectors: "My studio has become my own museum" (p. 166). His work is being placed
outside history, and by returning to Hungary he is not abandoning
art but reaffirming his belief in the artist's place in history. This
synthesis of the separation between the individual and history is
signalled finally in the novel by the anonymity to which Lavin returns; as the editor notes, the man disappears, perhaps killed, perhaps imprisoned, possibly even "He may have changed his name,
and so have become a man about whom we shall have news or shall
read" (p. 190). The ultimate fate of Lavin may be to be reduced to a
newspaper report, but the whole movement of the novel is to deny
the report a blithe objectivity as historical evidence. This sort of

historical fact ignores the dialectic between the individual and history.

The argument in the novel about the place of art in society is a complex one, as can be gauged from Berger's collection of art criticism written at the same time, *Permanent Red*. Certainly it would be unfair to suggest that Lavin's work (and indeed Berger's novel) is merely Socialist propaganda. As Lavin puts it: "I believe we have made a profound mistake whenever we have used our Marxism to make an arbitrary division between art that is for us (progressive art) and art which is against us (decadent art)" (p. 146). Historical perspective here is neither McEwan's view of the past as objectively different yet understandable in terms of an essential human nature, nor the propaganda that McEwan sees as arising from a denial of his view, propaganda, it might be pointed out, that McEwan locates in another novel by John Berger, *G* (McEwan, *Perspective*, p. 183). Rather, it is a Marxist view tempered by a rejection of dogmaticism: "Every attempt to turn an artist into a politician increases the contradiction [between the discipline of Communism and the discipline of art]. The more he understands his political significance as an artist—not as a politician—the less the contradiction will be" (p. 148). Again, the artist is involved in creating contemporary history, a position that by extension accepts both the difference between fiction and history, yet accepts their interdependence.

I am not myself interested in arguing the whole of Berger's case; I remain skeptical of the realist devices upon which the novel depends and its consequent failure to overtly analyze its fictivity— this is particularly pertinent given that both author and fictive editor share the same first name, and the status of the diary as evidence, as a "portrait," is unproblematically taken for granted. Moreover, the narrative progresses evenly in a manner quite unlike Lessing's, giving it a coherence which is certainly not as inevitable as the diarist himself suggests (*A Painter of Our Time*, p. 160). It is Lessing, not Berger, who uses the private chronicle to disrupt the narrative coherence of realism.

Nevertheless, in terms of theme if not of structure Berger does directly engage with the relativity of history and, as in Lessing, demonstrates a way in which the modern diary novel can question the objectivity of history without displacing facticity elsewhere. With regard to the diary as private chronicle Berger's novel argues for an interaction between the two poles of private subjectivity and public objectivity: "NOVEMBER 1. Self-knowledge . . . must always be balanced by an equal degree of world knowledge. . . . If the balance is unequal—too much self-knowledge produces the anarchist, and too much world knowledge the bureaucrat" (p. 155). Neither the private nor the public is privileged as the truth, and both are negotiable in terms of the other.

We can say, then, that both *A Painter of Our Time* and *The Golden Notebook* argue that, in the twentieth century, history is not waiting ready to be written but is something negotiated by individuals through their involvement with contemporary events; conversely, the individual inhabits a history that resides beyond the individual and with which the individual must come to terms. As private chronicles confronted by contemporary history, these diary novels dramatize a negotiation between areas of discourse, between private and public, subjectivity and objectivity, fiction and history, rather than passively record historical fact. They challenge the assumption that history is objective, that it resides beyond the realm of the private, and the reader who disagrees with them must nonetheless enter into the debate they set out. Indeed, what these novels suggest is that history itself is always subject to negotiation.

6

Writing the Self:
The Diary as Autobiography

The standard setting in which the fictive diarist is to be found is, according to H. Porter Abbott, "seated at a desk. On the desk there is ink, pen, and paper. The desk is in a room. The room contains at least two things: a window with a view and a mirror. It is a shabby room in a shabby house. The house is in a city" (*Diary Fiction*, p. 15). This seems predictable and unexceptional. The presence of the desk, the writing material, and the room result from the nature of the diarist's activity, and they can easily be naturalized by the reader as incidental and nonsignifying detail necessary for the writing of a diary. The window can be similarly naturalized for, if the diarist is in a room, it is likely he or she would have a window to look out of. However, the window certainly also has a metaphorical potential and offers a view onto the world from which the diarist has withdrawn in order to reflect in private on his or her position in the world. Hence the symbolic importance of the view being of the city, the locus of social activity.

Yet while the window might mark both the physical and metaphorical boundaries between public and private, between outside and inside, it is itself not neutral. While it offers a view of the outside, that view is restricted to the observer or diarist: it is a framed view. No omniscient view is possible, and, by withdrawing from the world, the diarist of necessity has only a partial view. The private has its effect on the public and, in looking out, the diarist is also looking inward.

In Eva Figes's *Nelly's Version*, for example, the diarist on arriving in a hotel room looks out not on an unfamiliar view but on one she has seen before: "I knew even before I walked across the floor and drew back the netting that I would look down on a lawn which had seen better days" (p. 12). In looking out, Nelly Dean merely sees a metaphorical reflection of herself, the self who has seen better days and from whom she has come to escape. Harold Atha in Rayner Heppenstall's *The Pier* has a more obviously restricted view of the outside world: "It is a measure of the closeness of their path to our house that I cannot see the path itself without almost pushing my nose against the window and, from as near as I dare go at the moment, can barely see three heads passing below" (p. 36). Here the physical restriction correlates with Atha's jaundiced view of others, a failure of perspective that leads Atha eventually to murder these neighbours for disturbing his peace. The view from the window is ostensibly an objective view of the world outside, yet it is framed by the subjective angle from which is viewed. The frame does not mark the limit of outside and inside but ensures that the view is both public and private at the same time.

The mirror, the second feature identified by Abbott as associated with fictive diary writing, is the counterpart of the window, ostensibly giving a private image of the diarist in the same way as the window ostensibly gives a view of the world outside. However, in the same way as the window is framed by the subjectivity of the observer and sets up a dialectical reversal, the frame of the mirror counteracts the privacy of self-analysis and gives a view of the subject as Other. It objectifies the self as an image to be studied, a reflection that, by reversing left to right, front to back, represents oneself as a new object. The frame once again does not mark a boundary between one sphere and another but "frames" the innocent observer: by a reversal, the observer has become self-incriminating. What the observer sees in the mirror is, as in the case of the window, a disturbing image constructed from a doubling or dialectic between private and public. This doubling offers a view of the self that has some resemblance both to one's public self and one's private self but is, because of the reversed image, neither the one nor the other:

I released my grip of the wardrobe door and it swung back, taking the image with it. I saw it full length now, the figure as it swung back like an object that had nothing to do with me, no hold on me. But it was obvious that I would have to exercise a firm grip on her. (Figes, *Nelly's Version*, p. 13)

What is being dramatized is the inherent instability in the way selfhood is constructed.

If Abbott is right about the conventional use of both window and mirror in diary fiction as a whole, then it is possible to correlate these with the autobiographical enterprise itself. Autobiography, insofar as it deals with the self (auto), the life (bio), and writing (graphy), must somehow negotiate between the conflicting dualities of private and public, inside and outside, the self and Other, writer and reader. Modern British diary fiction, as I hope to show in the four studies that follow, dramatizes the conflict inherent in autobiography in such a way as to deconstruct that very concept of an autobiographical selfhood, able to reflect on the world from a stable, rational position.

In John Fowles's *The Collector*, the narration is shared by two narrators, the kidnapper Frederick Clegg and the kidnapped Miranda Grey. Miranda's narrative is in the form of a diary and is embedded in Clegg's narrative, an embedding analogous to the way Miranda is incarcerated in his house. However, Clegg's narrative also acts as an editorial introduction to the diary and provides in its first part a retrospective context for the reading of the diary, as well as in its shorter second part an editorial afterword which brings the events up to date. *The Collector* therefore marks the point at which the (fictive) editor of the diary becomes a character of equal importance to the diarist.

Clegg is an autobiographer who fails to learn not only from his past but also from the process of autobiography. In the early part of his narrative he recounts how winning a fortune on the football pools leaves him essentially unchanged: "They still treated me behind the scenes for what I was—a clerk. It was no good throwing money around. As soon as we [he, his Aunt, and his cousin] spoke or did something we gave the game away" (p. 11). Clegg clearly defines himself as others see him, and there is no reflective consciousness of a difference between his present or writing self and the self written about. This seems, at least to a degree, to be the result of a lack of a developed and critical literacy on Clegg's part; he has trouble reading the book Miranda lends him (pp. 191 and 216) and his narrative style is colloquial and undeveloped: "I know my English isn't correct, but I try to make it correct" (p. 172). Thus Miranda comments: "What irritates me most about him is his way of speaking. Cliché after cliché after cliché, and all so old-fashioned, as if he's spent all his life with people over fifty" (p. 172). Miranda places Clegg in "the horrid timid copycatting genteel in-between class" (p. 172), a position Clegg himself seems to accept: "There was always class between us" (p. 42). Clegg therefore surrenders both to the use of literary conventions and to the social class Miranda and others place him in, features that Louis A. Renza associates with the "memoir" mode of autobiography: "The memoir-prone autobiographer uses language to declassify [i.e. make publicly available] information about his life: he uses language to apprehend his own life as an intersubjective phenomenon" ("The Veto of the Imagination," p. 280). The writer uses literary conventions and social categories to mitigate the split between a past self and a present self, thereby negating any self-reflection and possible psychological development. Clegg, at the end of his narrative, is thus able to contemplate repeating his past through a second kidnapping.

Clegg's ability is in taxonomy, both as a collector of butterflies and as a clerk in the Rates Office of the Town Hall, an ability that is dependent upon the inanimate nature of the materials he works with. Put another way, Clegg lacks the ability to perceive both himself and others as separate from himself and the categories he projects onto the world. Specifically, Clegg cannot come to terms with Miranda's sexuality, and, following her failure to seduce him, he resorts to categorical statements ("She was like all women, she had a one-track mind" [p. 113]) as well as to his photographs of her: "I could take my time with them. They didn't talk back at me" (p. 113). Moreover, we can argue that Clegg's lack of an actual father-figure has also played a part in his failure to move beyond Lacan's imaginary order and a belief in a unified self. Interestingly, Clegg's father died in a car crash when he was two and he was brought up by his aunt, according to Miranda, "Like Mrs Joe and Pip" (p. 194). The only adult to show him sympathy, Uncle Dick, died when he was fifteen: "he was as good as a father to me" (p. 8). Brought up in a matriarchal environment, Clegg is ego-centered and without a recognition of the Father, that exterior force which, Lacan argues, disrupts the imaginary identification with representations of the self. The converse argument here would be that Clegg's desire for union with a mother-figure has never been prohibited: "He has never had any parents, he's been brought up by an aunt. . . . I told him he was looking for a mother he'd never had" (p. 129).

Of course, there is a danger of overschematization and of giving too much weight to the type of amateur psychoanalysis Miranda here practices. However, a larger and largely supporting view is given by Dwight Eddins in "John Fowles: Existence as Authorship," in which Eddins identifies a similar conflict in Jungian terms. Eddins sees *The Collector*, and indeed Fowles's work in general, as a negotiation between contingency or hazard and the need to systematize contingency in a necessarily fictive way. The "existential quandary" for "Man" as the author of himself is in "reconciling his own ideations with the fortuitousness of existence. In humanizing this world he lies; in trying not to lie he is threatened by incoherence and chaos" (p. 205). Clegg as the figure of the Collector "imposes a static system of images on the world and then proceeds to live inside that system, denying the existential implications of contingency" (p. 205). Disturbingly, Eddins also locates the Collector impulse within Miranda Grey, with Clegg her psychological double: "She, also, has played the Collector by her smug accretion of upper-class values and assumptions that shut out the vitalizing powers of hazard" (p. 208). Eddins here quotes a comment made in the novel about her work as an art student: "You're saying something here about Nicholson or Pasmore. Not about yourself. You're using a camera. Just as *tromp-l'oeil* is mis-channelled photography, so is painting in someone else's style. You're photographing here. That's all" (p. 170). The same can be said of Miranda's frequent identification of herself and others with figures in literature.

Clegg, of course, is an actual photographer, using the camera in the same way as he uses autobiography, not to create but to fix movement and development; he remains a voyeur, unable to participate in human interaction. However, what leads Miranda beyond mere collection is the influence of "G.P." (George Paston), the artist. Through keeping a diary in the enforced isolation of Clegg's cellar, Miranda comes to realize the doubling of the subject position inherent in autobiographical writing: "I'm on edge, I'm nowhere near as calm as I seem (when I read what I've written). . . . What I write isn't natural. It's like two people trying to keep up a conversation" (*The Collector*, p. 138). In writing to herself, Miranda is writing to herself as reader, and she uses this doubling to mediate between the self-sufficient world in which Clegg lives and the world outside: "I felt I was going mad last night, so I wrote and wrote and wrote myself into the other world. To escape in spirit, if not in fact. To prove it still exists" (p. 167). Miranda recognizes the

necessary dialectic with an Other and, in making the split between
herself as writer and her self as object of the writing, Miranda
comes to see herself from G.P.'s perspective:

It's like the day you realize dolls are dolls. I pick up my old self and I see
it's silly. . . .
    I looked in the mirror today and I could see it in my eyes. They look
much older and younger. It sounds impossible in words. But that's exactly
it. I am older and younger. I am older because I have learnt, I am younger
because a lot of me consisted of things older people had taught me. All the
mud of their stale ideas on the shoe of me. (pp. 257, 258)

Writing about G.P. has brought Miranda to recognize the doubling
or the split subjectivity of the mirror and this ties in with Eddins'
view of G.P. as a Jungian constructive animus who provides
Miranda with "an existential Logos that deepens her capacity for
reflection and self-knowledge, without turning her into a dogma-
tist" ("John Fowles," p. 209). The dialectic between G.P. as animus
and Miranda as his anima is a creative dialectic necessary to art:
"Though 'collection' in the form of eidetic crystallization [generali-
zation and patterning] must occur in the very nature of things, its
life-denying properties would be continually minimized by the dialectic" (p. 210). Miranda becomes a critical subject, a subject who is
able to act on the world, specifically through her use of such contingent factors as the discovery of an axe or nail in her efforts to
escape.
    In terms of autobiography, therefore, Clegg remains an uncriti-
cal subject unable to see himself as Other: "I thought I was going
mad, I kept on looking in the mirror and trying to see it in my face.
I had this horrible idea, I was mad, everyone else could see it, only
I couldn't" (*The Collector*, p. 282). Miranda, on the other hand,
exceeds the psychotic world of Clegg by accepting the doubling
between self and Other, between her association with Clegg as
photographer and her difference, as suggested by Eddins, from him
as photograph. I cannot go so far as Eddins in accepting this as a
split between art and life, since I view the difference as the result,
rather than cause, of the autobiographical dialectic: it is internal to
the process of signification. However, I believe that Eddins is right
in positing G.P. as a third subject-position, an author-persona, toward which Miranda approaches at her death, though he is also a
figure of the general reader and the operation of language. G.P.
understands the dialectic and symbolizes, like the mirror and the
window, the conditions of autobiographical representation. He be-

comes, like the general reader, a figure through whom interpretation can be seen to circulate, that figure who emerges as a narrator in Fowles's *The French Lieutenant's Woman* to give competing versions of events. However, to the degree that the twin narratives concur about events in a realistic manner, *The Collector* is not in the end a radical investigation of interpretation; Miranda's death and the framing of her narrative within Clegg's curtails the movement away from character to text and the more radical strategies by which diary fiction has interrogated the notion of an autobiographical selfhood.

Like *The Collector*, Margaret Forster's *Private Papers* is a novel with two first-person narrators, one of whom keeps a diary. In Fowles, Miranda Grey's diary is sandwiched between the two parts of Clegg's narrative that act, as I suggested above, as a type of extended editorial foreword and afterword. In Forster, this quasi-editorial framing narrative is interpolated rather like the editorial commentary of John Berger's *A Painter of Our Time*, though the writer remains, like Clegg, an autobiographer in her own right.

The relationship between the narratives of *Private Papers* is fairly complex. The central narrator, Penelope Butler, a widow with three middle-aged daughters, writes the story of her children's lives: "this is not a memoir, not in any way an autobiography, though it will be inevitably that, in the process of setting the record straight, a great deal of my own life must be gone over. It is relevant, for a start, to say something about my own birth" (pp. 7–8). Alongside these private papers, she files copies of her diary entries for the period of composition: "Wasn't going to keep a diary this year, not when I'm trying to write this—whatever this other thing is, whatever it is I am trying to set down, sort out. But I can't survive without a diary too, it's a habit, maybe a bad one, but a lifetime's habit" (p. 32). Penelope Butler herself, therefore, writes two narratives, a retrospective memoir (which the history inevitably becomes) and a non-retrospective diary.

Beyond Penelope's narratives there is a second narrator, her eldest daughter Rosemary, who chances upon the papers while visiting her mother. Over a period of time, Rosemary reads through the papers, recording her reactions and her own version of events: "Oh *shit*—it's obvious I'm going to carry on reading this, I can't control my own curiosity. And this pencil is doing a St Vitus Dance in my hand with the need to put my own comments down" (p. 11). The device is somewhat clumsy, depending upon a kind of eighteenth-century, Richardsonian written stream-of-consciousness, yet it does result not only in an interpolated editorial commentary but in a set of diaristic and non-retrospective reading notes. In other words, Rosemary's narrative offers the reader of *Private Papers* a dramatized reading of Penelope's narrative.

As a whole, therefore, *Private Papers* is concerned more centrally than *The Collector* with the relationship between reader, writer, and the interpretation of reality. Penelope, the mother, envisages her narratives as having two different types of reader. Of her "autobiography," she writes:

Life does seem confusing and those who seek to impose a pattern upon it cannot expect to find it easy. I have to imagine a stranger as I write, I have to create a stern, judge-like figure to whom I must address myself, or, otherwise, this will disintegrate into a rambling, incoherent sequence of memories. (p. 7)

Although she has no thought to show her writing to anybody else, Penelope objectifies a reader in order to try to objectify her account, that is, in order to see her life from another's perspective. In contrast, she writes her diary for herself alone: "No need to imagine the judge-like figure, no need to fret over the fairness and truth of what I am saying. This is for me and I am friendly to myself and understanding, can say anything. Can say how upset I've felt today without despising myself" (p. 32). The diary is an act of overt self-indulgence in which Penelope attempts to disregard the distance between the writing subject and the written subject.

The main complication is, of course, the intervention of a real reader in the form of Rosemary: "Her papers are no longer private. I have made them my property, I have walked all over her memories, opinions and judgements, I have been a trespasser without mercy. And I have absolutely no regrets" (p. 252). Penelope's strategy of creating a judgemental figure in the memoir or of ignoring it in the diary fails when the works come into public circulation. Writing and its meaning are no longer controlled by the intentions of the writer, and the judge-like figure is revealed as a textual strategy for controlling the doubling of the authorial persona rather than a full acceptance of its consequences. Rather than being able to accept the full consequences of the split between a present self and a past self, consequences that would force on her a reinterpretation of the past, Penelope has mitigated the split by keeping two autobiographical narratives, one for the present and one for the past.

Penelope's failure is portrayed in terms of family relationships. In *The Collector*, Miranda Grey is able to move toward a self-awareness unavailable to Clegg because of the intervention of G.P., a symbolic Father-figure who reflects back on herself an image of herself as Other. In Penelope's private papers, however, the figure she invokes remains under her control and does not prevent her from deluding herself. Having grown up in a Children's Home without a father and having been widowed at the age of twenty-eight in the war, this symbolic Other has remained a figure of her imagination; like her namesake in the *Odyssey*, Penelope awaits the return of a husband, but unlike Ulysses, Oliver Butler never returns from the war. As Rosemary comments: "My father never died as far as my mother was concerned. Unfortunately" (p. 30). In his place Penelope creates merely a reflection of herself, an unconscious strategy that parallels her fantasy as a child in the Orphans' Home: "I would believe that somewhere my mother, like Ulysses, was fighting some war, was undertaking her own personal Odyssey, and would one day return to claim me" (p. 9). Again, as in the case of Clegg, we can argue that Penelope has identified not with a Father, through whom a true dialectic could operate, but with her self as wife/mother.

Significantly, as the memoir reaches the present, Penelope is led to self-doubt and the abandonment of her memoir. The two narratives, the memoir and the diary, collide: "I return again and again to those five short days and I see such significance in them. I cannot just abandon them to anything so slight and informal as a diary" (pp. 234–35). What forces Penelope to leave her account unfinished, at least according to Rosemary, is a traumatic five-day holiday in Florence with her three daughters:

What mother was doing, in the year 1984, was attempting to write an official family history. In the process she was shredding everyone's evidence but her own. . . . I think that she stopped writing after Florence, because on that holiday she realized she'd got it wrong. . . . We are three strong, assertive people to whom the Family is not sacrosanct. But what Mother came to appreciate was that perhaps this does not amount to failure on her or our part. (pp. 250–51)

Since none of her three daughters is by then still married, Penelope is forced to recognize, Rosemary suggests, that the family model she has tried to impose on her children may not be so absolute: "We've only 'failed' according to her original image, the image

I shall paint, to please her, when I tackle this painting I've prom-
ised her. Looked at from another point of view, we are successes,
surely" (p. 251). When her present intrudes into her story of the
past, Penelope's view of her family is shown to be an imaginary
representation and her children, like her writings, have become
something other than what she intended. Penelope can no longer
control events through language and the self-image she has constructed but must accept the operation of contingency. The fact
that she ceases to write shows the disrupting effect of such a realization on the notion of selfhood that underpins her autobiographical writings.

Which leaves us with the daughter's, Rosemary's, narrative. This
begins and ends the novel and to this extent gains the authority
of a framing editorial narrative. However, this narrative does not
claim the authority of, for instance, the editorial frame of Emma
Tennant's *The Bad Sister* where it is seen as a rationalist and specifically male discourse seeking to give meaning to the intuitive,
female discourse of Jane Wild's diary (see Chapter 8). Rather, while
Rosemary's narrative in *Private Papers* certainly questions the authority of Penelope's interpretation of the past by giving an alternative interpretation, at the same time it refuses to give a final
interpretation. Rosemary admits that her mother may not have
come to any awareness of failure: "Oh, fuck it. What the hell does it
matter? Maybe she hasn't finished, anyway. Any day she could be
resuming her narrative for all I know" (p. 251). But she herself still
refuses to simply destroy her mother's account: "Now what do I do?
Tear it all up? All these papers, plus my contribution? Wipe out
everything and, when the time comes, destroy the famous diaries,
scrapbooks and so forth? But if I did that, I'd be as domineering as
Mother, I'd be attempting to dictate history, too" (p. 251). Rosemary
is aware of the warnings of Orwell's *Nineteen Eighty-Four*, significantly the year in which Penelope has attempted her family history, and Rosemary's decision, therefore, is to deposit her papers
with her mother's: "I'll leave her precious papers where I found
them, but I'll leave my own too—it's only right that my perspective
should count for as much as hers" (pp. 251–52). The issue of interpretation is left for yet another reader to decide.

In *Private Papers*, then, Penelope's attempt to give a meaningful
account of her family's history founders on the kind of reader she
projects, an authoritative figure with whom there is no reciprocal
communication. He remains the composite Ulysses/Penelope figure
of her imagination, denying difference rather than increasing her

degree of self-awareness; he becomes, like the wig she has to wear temporarily, a way of framing or limiting the emergence of a second self: "Fearfully I looked in a mirror and, though I looked slightly odd, there was no doubt I also looked better. It was wonderful to see my face framed, as it had always been, by thick, wavy, bushy hair" (p. 57). This self-deception becomes obvious with the intervention of a real reader, Rosemary, who is able to offer an alternative interpretation. Rosemary has seen through the one-sided image of her father as Ulysses ("He was a War Hero and war heroes, once dead, were Brave and Strong and Masterful. Where, one wonders, are *his* private papers?" [p. 20]), and she is aware that neither history nor reality is objective. Rosemary, therefore, declines to replace her mother's view with her own and places the two narratives in parallel for any future reader to consider their relationship. We return, as in *The Collector*, to the view that there is no prior and authorizing autobiographical self and that meaning results from a dialectic or negotiation between different readers and different narratives. It is the possibility of private papers (as text) becoming public, of coming into circulation among a generality of readers, that makes it so.

Russell Hoban's novel, *Turtle Diary*, is far more schematic in its use of parallel narratives than is either *The Collector* or *Private Papers*. The novel is made up of fifty-three numbered sections, alternately narrated by William G. and Neæra H., two somewhat lonely inhabitants of London bed-sits, both in their mid-forties, who come together to conspire to steal three adult green turtles from an undersized tank in London Zoo and release them into the sea at Polperro in Cornwall. The focus is slightly stronger on William G., as the novel begins and ends with his narration, but, unlike in Fowles and Forster, neither character reads the other's narrative and the story is fully a joint enterprise. The twin narratives, therefore, structurally prefigure the interaction between the two protagonists and their own escape from isolation through working together to release the turtles.

Conversely, writing as a subject or theme is not so obvious as in Forster or Fowles. Neither of the narrators refers to their account as being written, though occasionally a section begins in an abbreviated diary style (p. 18); nor are there any datelines, though again some of the entries give the day of the week (p. 125). The diary element resides in the first place in the intercalated or periodic nature of the narratives. Although the actual sections are retrospective and do not involve a present-tense internal monologue, they are written at different points of the story.

A more important diary element is the notion of a diary as something private and generated by a self in isolation, for the movement of *Turtle Diary* is away from the inaction and sterility of an imprisoning selfhood toward an acceptance of contingency. William G., in suicidal mood, sees only himself reflected back at himself into infinity: "As the mind moves forward the self is pushed back, everything multiplies itself like mirrors receding laboriously into infinity" (p. 85). In this mood, William G. fails to see the enabling dialectic implied in his mirror reflection: he is trapped in an association with a past which must go on repeating itself, projecting itself into the future. William G. becomes a projection of his own father who killed himself by driving over a cliff into the sea (p. 86). He too, through divorce, has abdicated fatherhood, in his case in respect of the two daughters whom he has not seen for three years (p. 69). In *The Collector*, Clegg's father was similarly killed in a car crash and I suggested there that the death deprived him of a symbolic Father-figure which would stand for the operation of Otherness; Clegg fails to recognize any difference between his present and his past self, between the perceiving subject and the way others see him, and returns to his starting point in the repetition of a kidnapping. In *Turtle Diary*, however, there is no symmetry between actual father and symbolic Father, and identification with his father in contrast prevents William G. from perceiving the operation of difference. Thus William G., like Clegg, seems to see himself too fully as others see him. Neæra H. says of him: "That man at the bookshop has been seen as hopeless-looking long ago by someone, by himself as well, and his face has returned to that look" (p. 50). William over-identifies with a public, past self and is prevented from reacting to the present.

Neæra H. herself is in the same position: "My face does not look back at me now when I look into the mirror. That too is a return" (p. 50). And she too has become imprisoned in a static selfhood: "For years now I've had only myself and I must be economical with that self" (p. 73). Her identity has become fixed: "I could not have accepted the idea of myself as a stereotype when I was young but I can now" (p. 41). As in the case of Clegg and William G., Neæra H.'s overidentification with a past self has prevented her from seeing her present self as different, or even perhaps of seeing a present self at all: "I looked down at where I had been sitting in the square.

The bench was empty" (p. 78). The absence Neæra sees from her window is a reflection of her own lack of a private identity.

William G. and Neæra H. escape by acting together to release the turtles, an act that pulls them together despite themselves. They become part of a pattern of coincidences that, though neither will ever see the pattern (p. 156), will give a "new reality" (p. 50) to the world. They become involved in an action with an impetus outside themselves (p. 79) and which leads them briefly to escape a world in which the forward movement has been frozen, like the model village in Polperro or the model of a port at the Maritime Museum at Greenwich: "The past isn't connected to the future any more" (p. 69). They recognize something in the turtles which is missing in their own lives (p. 42), that the turtles have the possibility of a future, and it is this that draws them into a world of contingency and hazard; as William G. says: "I keep waiting for the phone to ring from that other world where the turtles are. It's not another world really, it's this one" (p. 121). They come to understand the imaginary nature of their overidentification with their past selves and the necessity of interaction and circulation.

In terms of the autobiographical act, then, William G. and Neæra H. are uncritical subjects who have identified too strongly with the way others see them, with their public selves—they have become locked into Renza's memoir-mode, a mode that mitigates the split between past self and present self. The active, yet destabilizing, difference inherent in autobiography has been lost. Both narrators identify with their fathers rather than recognize the Father as symbolic Other: William G. associates with his father's suicide, Neæra H. carries both the elaborate name her father gave her (p. 57) and a pebble as a reminder of him (p. 63). And both make a living from the imaginary nature of language: William G. works in a bookshop, Neæra H. writes children's stories. They are forced to break out of this mode by the imperative of freeing the turtles, an action that necessitates the projection of another self, one that might interact in the dialectic of a contingent world. Thus, after being given details by William G. of what they must do, Neæra H. reflects: "He spoke as if it was all really real and we were real people who were simply going to go ahead and do what we'd said we'd do" (p. 123). And in breaking out of the imaginary they are brought to understand the operation of the symbolic. Neæra H., for example, flings her pebble into the sea after stealing the turtles and later gives up writing her animal stories for children: "I was waiting for the self inside me to come forward to the boundaries from which it had long ago withdrawn. Life would be less quiet and more dangerous, life is risky on the borders" (p. 184). The border presupposes sameness and difference where meaning circulates, and with transgression of the imaginary comes a new sense of active and critical selfhood, a movement out of the safety of fixed stories.

The relationship between William G. and Neæra H. is a curious one, and its nonrealist textual manifestation marks it as a more radical appraisal of autobiography than either Fowles or Forster. They meet when Neæra H. comes into William's bookshop to read up about sea turtles: "I had the shocking feeling that here was another one of me locked up in a brain with the same thoughts. Me, what's that after all? An arbitrary limitation of being bounded by the people before and after and on either side" (p. 45). Again the border presupposes an area of dialectic, and it is arguable that in seeing themselves reflected in each other, William G. and Neæra H. in some way see objectified their imaginary self. Certainly, what happens in the course of the twin narratives is a repetition of their own private words in the text of the other: "I dreamt that nothing had a front any more. The whole world was nothing but the back of the world, and blank" (Neæra H., on p. 78); "It was as if the evening had reversed a giant devil-mirror with its picture of a world and I was silvered at the back of things, lost atoms speeding to infinity" (William G., on p. 107). Such parallels are indicators of like-thinking between William G. and Neæra H.; as Hoban himself puts it: "I thought of William and Neæra as two aspects of one entity" (Haffenden, *Novelists in Interview*, p. 137). Such parallels also emphasize the necessary doubling inherent in autobiography.

Yet, this technique of lexical repetition is quite unlike what happens in Fowles and Forster, where repetition of events serves to give a different and sometimes ironical meaning to those events. In Hoban, the technique of near and exact textual repetition works not just as a realist device which objectifies events but also as a transgression of realism. It questions referentiality, the border between text and reality. Of course, neither William G. nor Neæra H. reads the other's narrative, but for the reader the effect is a transgression of the assumption that there is a discrete and originating source of autobiographical narrative. The text itself transgresses the imaginary order of realism as the words that might be said to belong to Neæra H. find their way into William G.'s narrative.

We have in *Turtle Diary*, therefore, two autobiographical narratives which, contrasted, dramatize the autobiographical act, the doubling of the self that allows the subject to act on the world without passivity or a repetition of the past. But we also have, more firmly than in either Fowles or Forster, a text that operates on a third level. In Fowles the figure of the general reader, G.P., remained to the side of the dialectic between the writer and writer-as-reader as it appeared in Miranda's diary. In Forster, the figure of the general reader is dramatized within the text in the reading given to Penelope's narrative by her daughter Rosemary. In Hoban, however, though the green turtles act as the catalyst in the formation of a critical selfhood in William G. and Neæra H., there is no figure in the text through whom interpretation of their respective diaries circulates. This figure remains outside the text as the actual reader who must interpret the play of selfhood and the play of autobiographical narratives within the text. The text exceeds autobiography to the degree that the repetitions cannot be naturalized at the level of an autobiographical self—there is no stable point within the text from which to read the diaries. As autobiography, therefore, *Turtle Diary* scrutinizes the operation of the autobiographical act at a level at which the diaries themselves can no longer be read as the work of a fixed, stable autobiographical subject. The dialectic between the twin narratives scrutinizes not just the notion of selfhood but the intersubjective textuality consequent in writing the self.

Ann Quin's novel, *Passages*, employs a formal narrative scheme similar to that of Hoban's *Turtle Diary*. The narrative is divided equally into four sections, shared alternately between two first-person narrators, an unnamed woman and her similarly unnamed male travelling companion/lover. The woman's narrative is in the form of an internalized quasi-diary (see Chapter 7) and is comprised largely of fantasy impressions. The man's narrative is specifically a written account and takes the form of an annotated diary. The book is further divided into two halves, the first two sections, one by each narrator, covering events between June and August, the last two sections being parallel narratives of the events between July and December.

The events of the narrative concern a trip to an unidentified Mediterranean country in search of the woman's lost brother, and it becomes evident from the beginning that although there are two protagonists, the relationship between them is governed by an absent third figure:

Not that I've dismissed the possibility my brother is dead. We have discussed what is possible, what is not. They say there's every chance. No chance at all. Over a thousand displaced persons in these parts, perhaps more. So we move on. Towards. Away. Claiming another to take his place, as I place him in profile. Shapes suiting my fancy. Rooms with or without connecting doors. (p. 5)

This search involves balancing possibilities, such that the brother may or may not be dead, or that the couple may be travelling toward him or away. However, since the brother is not found, these possibilities are never resolved and there is no stable point of orientation: "Rooms with or without connecting doors." The brother's absence depends upon his difference from others (as symbolic Other), but that in turn proves to be dependent on the possibility of similarity and presence (of imaginary unity). For example, the woman's words, "Claiming another to take his place, as I place him in profile. Shapes suiting my fancy," admit both the brother's absence and his presence: she claims another to take his place as symbolic Other but can only do so by her recreation of similarities to her brother through "fancy." Her ability to substitute her companion for her brother makes her brother at once absent and present.

To give another example, the woman tries to identify her brother in a dossier of photographs shown her by the authorities: "I opened the folder of photographs. None of them bore any identity to each other, yet each had some singular aspect. A gesture. The stance of the body. Some showed only faces, faces in bad light, too much light. Out of focus" (p. 77). The photographs all show similarities with the brother, "some singular aspect," yet each body is different from the other: "None of them bore any identity to each other." Even the photograph that she carries of her brother is subject to this dissemination of identity: "The other photograph I no longer take out. Description adequate enough. But in that describing, at times, I lose track, as in relating a dream" (p. 62). We return to the "fancy," that operation of the imaginary which is dependent upon the absence of the brother and results in an undermining of the notion of identity and selfhood. It becomes evident that the novel itself is concerned with a search not for the missing brother but for some sort of pure identity, an identity that will overcome the dialectic between presence and absence, similarity and difference, the imaginary and the symbolic. The woman may have her "self" fixed by a photographic image—"A photo of myself against white railings, a look of fear in my eyes" (p. 78)—but this image can equally be that of an old woman tossing crumbs to gulls: "He took a photograph. She stood against the white railings" (p. 61).

The notion of selfhood is also examined in *Passages*, as in the other novels, by consideration of mirrors and their reflections: "Mirrors faced each other. As the two turned, approached. Slower in movement in the centre, either side of him, turning back in the opposite direction to their first movement. Contours of their shadows indistinct" (p. 25). Here the mirrors suggest that identity, the face that is recognizable in the mirror, is itself already a representation and depends both on similarity (recognizable features) and difference (the image is reversed, movement is reversed). Moreover, any perceived center, any possible fixing of an identity, can be projected into infinity: "The first mirror reflected in the second. The second in the first. Images within images. Smaller than the last, one inside the other" (p. 25). In *Turtle Diary*, this notion of mirrors facing each other was used to suggest a past, fixed identity, repeated into the future; overidentification with an imaginary past self had to be disrupted by a new identification with a symbolic current self in order to cope with a contingent and meaningless world. *Passages* is more radically disruptive in that it suggests that identity is always a process of repetition that can never be halted, a process nevertheless implicit in *Turtle Diary*: in the same way as William G. and Neæra H. depend upon a reflection of themselves in the other, so the woman and the man in *Passages* depend upon representations of themselves in photos and mirrors for a sense of selfhood. Indeed, like Willam G. and Neæra H., the characters are mirror images of each other, the same and yet different.

The difficulties of locating the boundaries of selfhood are extended by the use of parallel passages between the twin narratives. There are, again as in *Turtle Diary*, exact or near exact lexical repetitions. The couple undertake a train journey and the woman notes: "A passing line of birds. In the dust, a sudden stirring of wings, out of branches" (p. 9). In the man's narrative this is repeated as: "Rumble of wheels, a sudden stirring of birds rising out of trees" (p. 39). Although this seems to offer an objective recording of the same event, the repetition of "a sudden stirring" transgresses the realism of Fowles and Forster. This reliance of autobiography on writing becomes more obvious in other repetitions: "She stumbled over cripples in alleys, passage ways, knew they heard the rattle in her throat. The thought of knives thrown at her back" (p. 12); "I left and stumbled over cripples in passage ways, alleys. The thought of knives thrown at my back made me continually turn round" (p. 51). Here the same words are actually used to describe two different scenes. In the first, the woman is visiting a café; in the second, the man has just visited a prostitute, and indeed the alleys described are by no means even in the same city. Moreover, the woman talks about herself in the third person, highlighting the inherent doubling of self-reference in autobiography, the way that, in trying to write about the self, self-representation slips beyond the control of the writer.

We can say, therefore, that *Passages* is concerned not simply with the problem of fixing the self but with the problem of fixing presence through language. None of the characters and none of the places are given names, the diary dates are contradictory and largely nonspecific ("Mid-August" or "Saturday"), and, through the technique of parallel narratives, the same words are applied to different events. The first-person narrators exist, if they can be said to exist, in a world of shifting signifiers, in a world in which representations of the self, be it through photos, mirrors, or pronouns, can be attached with equal validity to other signifieds, other selves. Lacan's imaginary identification of the self with an image of its unity has been disrupted by the operation of the symbolic Other and the play of difference inherent in language. The search for the missing brother is bound to be frustrated since what they are searching for is something that has no substance but is revealed, like Lacan's notion of the unconscious, only in the interaction between the imaginary and the symbolic. The authority of the writer or even the writer-as-reader is disseminated, like identity, as the diaries move into the realm of the general reader where meaning is continually subjected to negotiation. The autobiographers are seen to be textually (de)constructed with no fixed identity.

Vicki Mistacco has analyzed something of the same effect in Alain Robbe-Grillet's *Topologie d'une cité fantôme*. Here Mistacco identifies instances of what she calls "repetition with difference" ("The Theory and Practice of Reading Nouveaux Romans," p. 388). For example, Robbe-Grillet's text alludes to previous textual elements and descriptions, allusions that amount to "counterfeit gestures toward reality" (p. 390). In the passage she quotes from Robbe-Grillet to demonstrate this, "the text displays its contradictory orientation by linking three distinct segments and by using one of these segments (the bridal shop) to lure the reader on to a 'new' development (the merchant) that both repeats and transforms a still earlier passage" (p. 391). Although Mistacco does not explicitly make the connection, one of the words in Robbe-Grillet that "draws the reader's attention toward the nonlinear functioning of the text" (p. 391) is in fact the word *passage*. Here it stands both for a passage of text and for a literal passageway in front of a row of shop windows. Quin's *Passages* predates Robbe-Grillet's novel by six years, but it is evident that Quin's literal use of "passage" to describe alleys similarly also carries the meaning of a passage of text: as the blurb puts it, "Ann Quin's new novel mirrors the multiplicity of meanings of the very word 'passages'." Indeed, the way in which we can here read "new novel" as *nouveau roman* does itself demonstrate the instability of meaning demonstrated by Quin's use of the same "passage" to refer in the parallel narratives to different events. The novel is concerned as much with the passage of the signifier as with the travels of the narrators.

Mistacco also points to the way in which repetition, with difference, figures in Robbe-Grillet through the use of mirrors. What is interesting here is their close link with the activity of the reader as he or she attempts to follow the passage of meaning:

Here is Robbe-Grillet's invitation to the reader to disseminate, unite, and disseminate again, to fragment then to bring together what is "impossible," only to break up the "synthesis" by realizing its potential for difference. Here is the inscription of mobility, of the incessant circulation of matter within and among texts. (pp. 395–96)

Of course, to recognize the circulation of meaning inherent in writing the reader must start from the position of the traditional reader, "striving for a reassuring reconstruction of reality" (p. 396); but to take pleasure in the text the reader must become one who rejoices in transgression. As Mistacco puts it, "the reader may become positively and productively schizoid" (p. 397).

The notion of schizophrenia and madness is one that is pertinent to *Passages* by the way in which the identity of the narrators is disseminated through the use of photographs, mirrors, and the paralleling of passages. The man, for example, keeps not just a diary but annotates it with secondary observations: "How she watches me. God how she watches herself watching. However if no one observes me I have to observe myself all the more" (p. 31).

Identity is based on a shifting subjectivity. Mistacco suggests that such texts which refuse to close the operation of meaning require new types of reading conventions; this may be so, but what *Passages* also suggests is that this schizophrenia is inherent in writing the self in autobiography. Moreover, this schizophrenia is transferred to the reader by the fact that the word *passage* itself can have a number of meanings, an unavoidable instability of text that makes it open to contrary readings. We return to the third subject position with regard to autobiography whereby the author is replaced by the reader, whereby intention is replaced by reception.

Elizabeth Wright, using a triangular scheme based on Lacan, suggests that this third position is that of the deconstructionist reader:

The authorial ego, seen as omniscient by past critics, would initially be at the top of the triangle. The so-called competent reader (or whatever idealization is applied to the concept "reader"), he who tries to recover a stable meaning, even if he allows that there might be several such stable meanings, would be in position 2. . . . The third position is the deconstructionist's position, which is that of a reader who discovers instabilities in both these positions and who produces an innovative reading which takes into account the problematic relationship between author and text, and between reader and text, in terms of their intentional perspectives. ("Modern Psychoanalytic Criticism," pp. 129–30)

The authorial ego inhabits the imaginary order of intentionality. The competent reader is that reader who refers his or her reading back to a stable point such as the author; it is the domain of the writer-as-reader or the old-fashioned "classical" psychoanalytical critic who accounts for the mismatch between intention and reception, the operation of the symbolic Other, in terms of the author's psychology. The deconstructionist reader, however, escapes from one or the other idealization by adopting a position that utilizes at another level the dialectic between the first two positions, between the imaginary and the symbolic. Moreover, as Wright goes on to point out, we are not talking here purely of the niceties of poststructuralism, but of the basic relationship between writing and reality: "These perspectives are upon reality. What issues from the conflict of readings of the text is the question of which perspective is most viable, how reality is to be viewed. . . . Three 'readers' are trying out representation after representation in order to test their view of the world" (p. 130). In *Passages*, the narrators are searching not so much for the missing brother but for the conditions in which their narratives may transcribe pure presence. Their search is, thus, doomed by the dialectical nature of the autobiographical subject; yet the course of their search and their testing of contrary representations of the world offer the actual reader autobiographies that, if they do not give a fixed point for interpretation, at least challenge readers to offer their own readings, their own perspectives. The twin narrators operate both as writer and as the writer-as-reader, but it is for the reader of *Passages* to account for this in terms of the operation of the language of the text. It is at this point that the diarist and the reader have to face the common problem of the relation between writing and reality.

What I hope I have demonstrated in this chapter is that those diary novels that are constructed from twin first-person narratives all rely to varying degrees not merely on a dialectic between the narratives but on a third position, that of the general reader through whom competing interpretations circulate and are negotiated. In Fowles's *The Collector*, that figure was the shadowy figure of G.P., the symbolic Other who resided on the margins of the text and who enabled Miranda to come to realize the dialectic implicit in her own self-representation. In Forster's *Private Papers*, the reader was dramatized in the conflicting interpretation given to Penelope's narratives by Rosemary, yet another interpretative shift being left to a future reader. Hoban's *Turtle Diary* again showed both the necessity for Neæra H. and Willam G. to recognize the autobiographical dialectic in order to overcome a disabling fixing of self, but it also brought the actual reader more fully into the dialectic by a disruptive repetition of text. This transgression of autobiographical intention was the most disruptive in Quin's *Passages,* where characters and reader alike are unable to contain the shifts of meaning inherent in the operation of language. To the degree that the readers are unable to arrive at a final interpretation, they are brought to realize the dialectical nature not simply of the narrators but of themselves as readers. The text offers an account of identity formation but does so in such a way as to set up a further dialectic, that between the reader and the text. The problems of selfhood become operative not merely within the narratives but at the level of text as a working model of the first dialectic. Reading becomes, therefore, a self-reflexive process, one in which readers of these novels are brought to face an image of themselves within the

7

Writing at Sea:
The Fictive Sea Journal

Because Britain is an island and the British a seafaring nation, the sea journal has always been an important part of the British diary-writing tradition. Tracing a line back to the earliest of captain's logs, sea journals have been kept by navigators, scientists, ambassadors, and emigrants. Almost four hundred years ago Francis Bacon noted: "It is a strange thing that in sea-voyages, where there is nothing to be seen but sky and sea, men should make diaries, but in land-travel, wherein so much is to be observed, for the most part they omit it" (p. 54). Even today many a British holiday diary begins with the crossing of the English Channel.

Such diaries have, however, been not only written but read and have thus provided subsequent diarists with a model to copy and adapt. Such diaries have also, at least since the late seventeenth century, provided fiction writers with a recognizable nonfiction form to imitate, and indeed the first fictive diary to appear in Europe, Robinson Crusoe's journal (1719), is clearly influenced by the form of the two sea journals that provided Defoe with the source of his story.[1]

There are, of course, complex historical reasons why writers of fiction imitate the forms of other types of writing, and one might cite the use of the diary in the early novel as a link between the development of a new form of realism and the growing habit of diary keeping among the novel-reading public. In any historical analysis one would also have to consider the rise of diary publishing, somewhat surprisingly postdating the use of the diary in fiction. But my main concern is with the use of the sea journal in modern fiction, and here we can observe more clearly its attractions for the writer. The modern writer is, in general, concerned with a psychological examination of character, and the first-person of the diary form provides a way of stressing changes in perception, of analyzing present states of mind and contrasting them with subsequent reflections. More specific to the sea journal, a sea voyage provides a hazardous environment in which character can be tested, a hazardous and often alien environment that correlates typically with a crisis in the diarist's life. It is a rite of passage, often physical as well as metaphorical. The sea voyage also provides a solitude in which the diarist, removed from his or her daily routine, can reflect upon the way of life left behind and mentally prepare for a return. And a voyage has the advantage to the writer of consisting of a discrete series of events with a beginning, a middle, and an end, although novelists in practice tend to concentrate on either the start of a voyage or its conclusion.

The present chapter compares five such fictive sea journals, William Golding's *Rites of Passage* and its immediate sequel *Close Quarters*, Robert Nye's *The Voyage of the Destiny*, B. S. Johnson's *Trawl*, and Malcolm Lowry's short prose piece, "Through the Panama." Of course comparison tends to stress difference rather than similarity, and it should be pointed out that it is not my purpose to outline a definition of the sea journal as a subgenre of diary fiction, even were such a definition tenable. More importantly, I should stress that, while my four authors may have been greatly influenced by the possibilities of the sea-journal form for the examination of character, my own concern will be to place character portrayal second to an examination of the different ways these authors explore the use of a nonfiction form for the purposes of fiction. This approach has been partly determined by the methodology adopted, all four texts showing more similarities in respect of characterization than differences, but also because to restrict oneself to, say, Golding's notion of good and evil or to B. S. Johnson's obsession with isolation would be to ignore the important way each of these texts explores a certain limit of the way in which diaries can be imitated. In short, my approach will be more strictly formal and will concentrate on the text as a fictive document, that is, as a fictional framing of a nonfiction mode; it will look at such matters as the diarist's consciousness of the act of writing and, an unavoidable concern of the journal form, the dating of the entries.

To begin with Golding's *Rites of Passage* would suggest that of all four authors Golding is the most conservative, a model from which the others depart, and to a large extent this is true. Certainly the central concern of this novel is a traditional one, the hero's growth into maturity. The rites of passage alluded to in the title are not only the rites performed on the sea voyage at the crossing of the equator but also the painfully necessary testing of the young hero in his passage into adulthood. Edmund Talbot, a young man of high birth, sets sail in the early nineteenth century for "the Antipodes" to take up a position as assistant to the Governor of New South Wales. His ship is an obsolete man-of-war, and his daily account records how he becomes embroiled in the stormy relationship between the autocratic and anticlerical Captain Anderson and the grotesque yet dedicated Parson Colley, a relationship that results in the parson's death. Talbot's initial assessment of both captain and parson dramatically collapses along with his previous rationalist certainties on the posthumous discovery of a confessional letter written by Parson Colley. Good and evil are recognized as so entwined that they cause Talbot a harsh, if still provisional, reassessment not only of the individuals concerned but of the nature of a society, for which the ship acts as a microcosm.

Yet to stress this aspect of the work is to mask a way in which the text represents a limit of the modern fictive sea journal. For *Rites of Passage* is an impressive recreation of the fictive diary as it had developed by the time in which the novel is set, even to the extent of imitating the literary language of the time. In *The Diary Novel*, Lorna Martens demonstrates how an intermediate form, some way between the epistolary novel of the early eighteenth century and the diary novel as it later emerged, developed in the later eighteenth century.[2] We can see the beginnings of this form in Richardson's *Pamela* (1740), which, though it is mainly an epistolary novel, moves toward the diary novel when Pamela is imprisoned in Lincolnshire; she continues to write to her parents at periodic intervals despite the fact that she has no way of conveying her letters to them. Lorna Martens describes this intermediate form as the letter journal, a journal written specifically for someone other than the diarist, and in *Rites of Passage* we find Talbot addressing his journal to his "Honoured godfather": "With those words I begin the journal I engaged myself to keep for you" (p. 3).

Strange as this may appear to the modern reader, in the eighteenth century the notion of a journal did not necessarily mean, as
it does now, that the daily entries were written solely for the diarist's own eyes, and it was common practice to keep a journal as a
form of correspondence—witness Swift's *Journal to Stella* (1710–
1713), written for Hester Johnson and her companion Miss Ding-
ley, or Boswell's *London Journal* (1762–1763), posted in weekly
parcels to his friend John Johnston. The term "journal" meant a
record of each day's events, hence the term "journalism."

Nevertheless, though the letter-journal novel incorporates a specific addressee in the manner of the epistolary novel, the presence
of such a figure, according to Martens, does not influence the style
and content of the work to the same degree as in the multivoiced
epistolary novel. The epistolary novel can set different versions of
events side by side in order to demonstrate a character's insincerity or lack of self-awareness; the letter-journal novel by contrast
does not presuppose a reply. Thus in *Rites of Passage*, despite the
inclusion of some rather heavy-handed irony, Golding finds it necessary to include Parson Colley's own letter journal to draw attention to the unreliability of Edmund Talbot's account. Talbot inserts
the "Colley Manuscript" in his own journal as an act of "natural
justice" (p. 183), as evidence of his own callousness and another's
sincerity. In so doing, of course, Talbot also demonstrates his own
new-found sincerity.

Golding also keeps to his letter-journal model in his choice of
character. According to Lorna Martens, the central character in the
letter-journal novel is a young, virtuous woman whose thoughts
and emotions do not admit of much variation. Hence, "It is not her
thoughts that are of primary interest . . . but rather the events that
befall her" (*The Diary Novel*, p. 79). The fictive letter journal is
concerned more with the past-tense relating of events than with a
present-tense examination of thoughts. Of course, Edmund Talbot
is no virtuous young woman, and much of the interest of the novel is
in how he is shaken out of the naive confidence he derives from his
social position. Nonetheless, *Rites of Passage* is quite unlike modern diary fiction in that there are few, if any, moments of self-
reflection for their own sake. Talbot's moments of introspection
are limited to those of the fictive letter journal, that is, they are
what Martens describes as "either reactions to past events, or
speculations about possible future events" (p. 82). The result of this
is that Golding, if he has to give a representation of heightened
emotion, must, like Richardson in *Pamela*, have his hero some-

what awkwardly transcribe his thoughts in the midst of events. Immediately after reading Colley's letter, Talbot reaches for his journal:

Why Edmund, Edmund! This is methodistical folly! Did you not believe you were a man of less sensibility than intelligence? Did you not feel, no, *believe*, that your blithely accepted system of morality for men in general owed less to feeling than to the operations of the intellect? Here is more of what you will wish to tear and not exhibit! But I have read and written all night and may be forgiven for a little lightheadedness. (pp. 183–84)

Talbot must not only think such thoughts but write them as he thinks them, and the form of the novel pulls against the thrust of the message. If feelings are to be allowed to affect the intellect, Talbot the rationalist cannot go so far as to abandon the intellectual pursuit of writing.

In *Close Quarters*—the immediate sequel to *Rites of Passage*—Edmund Talbot keeps a second diary, this one, however, not addressed to a specific addressee but kept for his eyes alone: "This is not a continuation, but a new venture. When this is filled with an account of our voyage I mean to keep it for myself and no one else" (p. 3). This is indeed a new venture for formally it departs from the letter-journal model and develops into more of a nineteenth-century private and introspective nonfiction diary. Formally, therefore, *Close Quarters* makes clearer Talbot's rite of passage into a new century, a century that, with the ending of the Napoleonic Wars, will radically question the social position Talbot is so keen to defend: "The peoples of Europe and our own country were now set free from the simple and understandable duty of fighting for their king and country. It was an extension of that liberty which had already turned ordered societies into pictures of chaos" (p. 55). As a metaphor for this change, the obsolete man-of-war in which Talbot is sailing becomes even more unseaworthy, a metaphor paralleled more subtly by the break-up of the letter-journal narrative as the record becomes more introspective (Talbot takes up writing Romantic poetry after his brief encounter with Miss Chumley, "an ingenuous opening of my heart to the page" [p. 280]) and more retrospective ("I was often writing of the past when much was happening at the moment" [p. 279]). Talbot is charting the evolution of narrative form, culminating in the fully retrospective and seemingly more objective narrative of the nineteenth-century realist novel: "Honesty compels me to promise a plain narrative at some later date which will see the voyage ended and which narrative shall be my 'book three.'" (p. 280). This is the final book of Golding's trilogy, the memoir novel *Fire Down Below*. In Britain, the nineteenth century historically saw a rise in the private diary but a comparative abandonment of diary fiction until the last years of the century under the influence of the French *journal intime*.[3]

In *Rites of Passage*, then, Golding not only imitates the language of Augustan and Romantic literature, he also imitates closely the form of the fictive letter journal, both in his use of a specific addressee and in his stress upon intrigue rather than character depiction. To put it more exactly, although Talbot within the novel writes a letter journal, Golding himself does not so much imitate the nonfiction letter journal as imitate the traditional letter-journal novel, a tradition appropriate to the time in which the story begins. There is, thus, a hidden depth to the form of *Rites of Passage* paralleling the hidden depths that scupper Talbot's social and political perceptions, and by using a fictional rather than a nonfiction model, Golding produces a work that is both traditional and yet pushes the fictive sea journal to a new limit. Though *Rites of Passage* is on balance a traditional modernist examination of consciousness, it nevertheless engages with the postmodern interest in the intertextual relationship between texts, the breakdown of the discrete boundaries between "original" works. Once again, it is the notion of wholeness and individuality that is being questioned.

At first sight, Robert Nye's *The Voyage of the Destiny* would seem, like *Rites of Passage*, to be modelled on the eighteenth-century letter journal. Sir Walter Ralegh, sailing home from his final abortive search for gold in Central America, records daily events for the benefit of his young son, Carew. Yet despite the use of a specific addressee, the work is set in the early seventeenth century, predating the development of the letter journal. At the same time, Nye's novel employs many of the resources of modern diary fiction. Having kept a journal of the voyage out, Ralegh scraps it because it avoids his true thoughts and feelings. He begins afresh:

I wrote that journal to and for myself. Now I write to you. For you, Carew, my son. And what I write will not be exactly a Journal. What will it be? I don't know. I am writing it partly to find out. It will have to be something like the truth. But more than a Journal, and less. No giant or god stuff. But some kind of confession. The story of my days past and the story of my days present. What I was and what I am. What and who. For you, Carew, who do not really know me. (p. 9)

As we have seen, this use of an addressee in diary fiction is not new, though it is enough of a departure from the modern expectation that a diary is private for Nye to need to justify such a departure early in the narrative. Of more interest, however, is the notion of Ralegh's journal as a confessional, a recounting not just of days present but of days past, and Ralegh goes so far as to call this retrospective aspect an autobiography: "I turn again to examine my own mortality by autobiography" (p. 150). Such a statement is both anachronistic (the term "autobiography" dates from the nineteenth century) and not part of the letter-journal tradition (autobiography is notably absent from Talbot's journal in *Rites of Passage*, though it becomes the form of the final part of Golding's trilogy, *Fire Down Below*). Moreover, the other side to the notion of a confessional, the statement of a present state of mind, is likewise a modern development in diary fiction, and Nye's use of a modern English prose to represent an introspection that derives not simply from the events of the immediate past, as in *Rites of Passage*, is typical of the way he employs the resources of the modern diary novel to write a historical novel. *The Voyage of the Destiny* is a work very different in its conception from Golding's faithful recreation of a past language and a past narrative form.

Such a difference can also be seen if we compare the two novels as fictive documents. Both works show a concern for the text as a book, as a physical and potentially subversive document. Edmund Talbot's letter journal ends with him vowing to lock his book for the last time, sew it in sailcloth and stow it away in a locked drawer (p. 278). Talbot will continue his record of the voyage, but in a book kept less secret from prying eyes: "Of course my journal will continue beyond this volume—but in a book obtained for me . . . from the purser and not to be locked" (p. 264). Ralegh's journal is similarly dangerous and also has to be kept secret, being hidden prior to his imprisonment in the Tower of London: "I shall not write down the present provenance of all that I had written formerly. . . . Sufficient to say that those papers were safely secreted before I left Broad Street on my way to be betrayed" (p. 361). The diary as fictive document has a potential to influence the plot.

Yet while both *The Voyage of the Destiny* and *Rites of Passage* are clearly concerned with the diary as a physical document, they differ in two respects. The first concerns dating. The diary entries in *The Voyage of the Destiny* begin on 13 February 1618 and are dated throughout the text, the last entry being for 28 October, the day before Ralegh's execution. In *Rites of Passage*, on the other hand, the entries are denoted according to the days of the voyage, and neither the year nor the day of the month are given in the text. The exact dating of *The Voyage of the Destiny* functions not only to set the period in which events of the story occur but to offer a degree of historical authenticity to the journal itself. Only to a degree, of course, since much of the tale is fabricated, but it would seem that the inclusion of a historical figure as diarist places an imperative upon the novelist to date accurately known historical events. *Rites of Passage*, however, has no such imperative since no historical figures are involved and, though Golding is scrupulously accurate as regards his period setting, the vagueness of the dating in the diary is an indication that the novel is a fiction with a historical setting rather than a historical novel.

Documents included in the fictive journal have a function similar to that of the dateline. Sir Walter Ralegh includes many documents likely to be of use to his son in judging the actions of his father; for example, he includes the warrant for his arrest, an insincere apology to the King for the failure of his expedition, and a lying letter to the Privy Council written by the ship's chaplain. Edmund Talbot, by contrast, includes only one document, the letter journal written by Parson Colley. Of course, in both Ralegh's and Talbot's journals the documents are framed by the diarist's entries, and reasons are given in both narratives for the inclusion of such documents. Their main difference lies in their formality—the parson's letter in *The Voyage of the Destiny* is one of a series of formal documents concerned with the public life of Ralegh, such documents being a way in which Nye can draw attention to the contrast between the man and his fame. The parson's letter in *Rites of Passage* is a private document, a document in fact more sincere than Talbot's preceding diary entries. Both parsons' letters serve to contrast the sincerity of the framing narrative, but in the case of *The Voyage of the Destiny* the public nature of the documents has the additional function of reinforcing the factual authenticity of the tale. Again, as in the case of the exact dating, what the historical novel surrenders in formal authenticity it gains in historical authenticity, and compared with *Rites of Passage*, *The Voyage of the Destiny* as a historical novel marks a very different limit to the fictive sea journal. As I argued in Chapter 5, Nye and Golding have different strategies with regard to the facticity of history.

To categorize B. S. Johnson's *Trawl* as a sea journal will need some initial justification for, unlike *Rites of Passage* and *The Voyage of the Destiny, Trawl* has no dated entries. Instead, the action of the voyage is narrated in a form of stream-of-consciousness, a mental recording of sights and sounds as they occur:

I sit in the wireless room, with Molloy. He says little, Molloy, but what he does have to say is interesting. Of being shipwrecked on a desert island, yes, in the Pacific, in the war, and being rescued by a negro. The chair I sit in rocks and slithers to the limits of its restraining tether. Apart from this movement, being in the wireless room with Molloy is not like being on a ship at all, here is the place on the ship least like being on a ship. (pp. 113–14)

Of note here are the deictic references, the simple present tense of "I sit" and "he says" and the close adverbs "here" and "this," markers that are appropriate to the historic present of some forms of diary writing, as in the first Mass-Observation Day Survey analyzed in Chapter 3: "I curl up in a low armchair. Listening to wireless. Going to get dark early tonight. Raining. We sit in the twilight" (Calder & Sheridan, p. 7). However, *Trawl* makes no mention of the act of writing, and the notion of the text as a physical object, noted in both Golding and Nye, is absent.

Nevertheless, there is a case to be made for *Trawl* as a journal, at least in part. In formal terms the narrative of *Trawl* is divided fairly strictly between a first-person present-tense description of the narrator's voyage on board a fishing vessel and a past-tense recollection of events in the narrator's life, events recalled while he lies seasick on his bunk. The sections concerning the voyage occupy roughly two-fifths of the text, and from information supplied in the text we can calculate the date of most of these sections—for example, the voyage begins on Thursday 13 October and hence the final day of fishing, given as the fifteenth day of the voyage, can be dated as Thursday 27 October. Thus, although no full day is described, *Trawl* shares the periodic narration of the diary.

Lorna Martens calls this type of narration "quasi-diary fiction" (*The Diary Novel*, p. 136), a type of narration that allows the author to concentrate on the psychology of the protagonist without being encumbered by the conventions of writing. If we can see the development of the letter journal in Richardson's *Pamela* as a means by which the consciousness of the isolated protagonist can be externalized, then the movement from the fictive diary to a stream-of-consciousness technique, as occurs between the diary ending of Joyce's *A Portrait of the Artist as a Young Man* and *Ulysses*, marks a devel-

opment in the same direction. In other words, the transition between the epistolary novel and the diary novel marked by the letter
journal, and the transition between the diary novel and the stream-
of-consciousness novel marked by Martens's quasi-diary, were both
attempts to discover new ways of depicting a character's thoughts.
By retaining periodic narration, however, the quasi-diary can examine psychological changes over a longer period of time than is
usual in the stream-of-consciousness novel.[4]

The modern writer of diary fiction thus has a range of options for
combining events and narration. The protagonist may be tied to
the writing desk, recounting recent events:

I have just come from the passenger saloon, where I have sat for a long
time with Summers. The conversation is worth recording, though I have
an uneasy feeling that it tells against me. (*Rites of Passage*, p. 124)

the protagonist may be still at the desk but recording events occurring simultaneously:

The swabbers out there are cleaning our decks of the blood. I can hear the
brutes singing. Singing! They like their work, evidently. (Better than I
like mine. Who can clean these pages? . . .). (*The Voyage of the Destiny*, p.
201)

or the protagonist may abandon the desk altogether and go up and
about on deck:

So up, up the companionway, the ladder, holding the handholes in the
teak sides tightly, through the hatch hanging on to the vertical brass bar,
right: what's this on the cream walls of the alleyway, brown, smearing the
painted surface? · · Blood, yes, it's blood, it can't be human, can it, no, it's
where they brush, from the gutting, where their bloody smocks smear
against the sides. (*Trawl*, p. 32)

In *Rites of Passage*, the narrator reflects as he writes of the immediate past; in *The Voyage of the Destiny*, the narrator writes of the
present as he reflects; and in *Trawl* the narrator just thinks, without the acknowledgement that what we read is a written representation of thought.

But if *Trawl* works at the quasi-diary limit of the fictive sea
journal, it also explores the limit of diary fiction as autobiography.
The sections framed by the quasi-diary narrative are autobio-

graphical reminiscences, attempts by the narrator to analyze the events of his past. He has undertaken the voyage "to shoot the narrow trawl of my mind into the vast sea of my past" (p. 11), to try, through a physical isolation, to understand the causes of his emotional isolation. His voyage is both physical and emotional, the green bile of his sea-induced vomit symbolizing the purging of his past. As he is told by the old trawlerman when he first comes on board: "You'll be sick. I told him I had tablets for seasickness. They'll be no use to you, he said, You'll be sick until you bring up your green bile, you've got to bring up the green bile that's been there maybe since you were a child. And once that green bile's gone, you'll be all right" (p. 118).

Sir Walter Ralegh in *The Voyage of the Destiny* is similarly seasick: "I threw up every gobbet of my self-esteem, the bitter-as-wormwood dregs of my life and my hopes, whatever secretions remained of a long feast on nothing" (p. 204). Indeed, the intertwining of past and present in Ralegh's journal produces a medley of voyages paralleling those in *Trawl*:

> This book, I see now, is the log of three voyages.
> The first: The voyage of the *Destiny*. Set in the present time. . . .
> The second: The voyage of my history. The tale of my life and fortunes. . . .
> The third voyage is the most difficult to define. . . . "*The Voyage of the Destiny*." That's my third voyage. The true task. (p. 254)

In this third voyage, the novel *The Voyage of the Destiny*, Nye has Ralegh briefly break out of the naturalistic mode to signal a kind of metaphysical, metafictional awareness. Ralegh in *The Voyage of the Destiny* is, after all, in the uncomfortable position of being both fact and fiction. But although such an awareness is absent from Johnson's narrator, its absence is a product of a more radical approach to the dividing line between fiction and autobiography.

To begin with, Johnson's narrator is far less certain of the facts of his past than Nye's Ralegh, whose problem is precisely that he can neither forgive nor forget (p. 127). For the narrator of *Trawl*, the problem of making sense of his past is compounded by a struggle to remember what his subconscious has suppressed: "I must think of it all, remember it all, it must be everything, otherwise I shall certainly not understand, shall have no chance of understanding, that I most desire, that I am here for" (p. 17). The bringing up of the green bile.

Nevertheless, a biography does emerge, and it is in respect of this that *Trawl* most strongly explores the frontier between fact and fiction. For unlike the narrator of *Rites of Passage* or *The Voyage of the Destiny*, the narrator of *Trawl* is unnamed. To be sure, an unnamed narrator is not unique to *Trawl,* but in the absence of a name the text might be expected to indicate whether or not the narrator is the author—by, for instance, setting the narrative in a historical period or by giving the narrator a different gender. In *Trawl*, there is no such indication, and this leaves an uncertainty as to how the text is to be read, as to whether or not we are reading the autobiography of B. S. Johnson. Recourse to other works by Johnson is inconclusive since they too share this uncertainty, and in the absence of a biography we are left with an ambivalence. Johnson himself claims that *Trawl* is a nonfiction novel: "It is a novel . . . what it is not is fiction" (*Aren't You Rather Young to Be Writing Your Memoirs*, p. 14); but even the nonfiction novel must associate itself with the writer's life for it to be read as such. And there is the additional problem that *Trawl* uses fictional strategies such as a vagueness of dating (as in *Rites of Passage*, no year is given) or the stream-of-consciousness technique. In short, *Trawl* cannot be read with ease either as fiction or as autobiography: it is an indeterminate case and as such it explores the very basis of the fictive journal form, the embedding of a nonfiction form in a fictional frame. Unlike *Rites of Passage* or *The Voyage of the Destiny*, *Trawl* relaxes that frame.[5] It is left to Malcolm Lowry's "Through the Panama" to shatter the frame completely.

If B. S. Johnson creates a certain biliousness in the reader by refusing to name his narrator, Malcolm Lowry shipwrecks us in a whirlwind of identities. "Through the Panama" has the subtitle "From the Journal of Sigbjørn Wilderness" and a number of the entries seem to confirm that the diarist is indeed Wilderness: "Sigbjørn Wilderness (pity my name is such a good one because I can't use it) could only pray for a miracle" (p. 40). However, this speaking of himself in the third person suggests a certain distancing from himself, an inability to accept an identity; it suggests that the diarist is indeed a "seaborne" (Sigbjørn) wilderness of competing identities:

Plight of an Englishman who is a Scotchman who is Norwegian who is a Canadian who is a Negro at heart from Dahomey who is married to an American who is on a French ship in distress which has been built by

Americans and who finds at last that he is a Mexican dreaming of the
White Cliffs of Dover. (p. 96)

What seems to have occurred is that in making his voyage from
Canada to Europe via the Panama Canal, Wilderness has begun to
see himself as Martin Trumbaugh, the hero of the novel he is writing and who is making a similar voyage (p. 27). To complicate matters further, Martin Trumbaugh himself is a writer who in turn
becomes caught up in his own novel (p. 27). It is therefore not too
surprising that Trumbaugh not only also has a wife called Primrose
but shares much of Wilderness's own personal history (p. 38). By
making the narrator of "Through the Panama" a novelist, Lowry
adds another dimension to the examination of the past dealt with in
both *The Voyage of the Destiny* and *Trawl*; and this paralleling of
authorial and fictional autobiography dramatizes the duality of the
autobiographical element inherent in the fictive journal form, its
generic status as both fiction and nonfiction.

Yet while Trumbaugh is to some extent an *alter ego* of Wilderness, there is an implicit suggestion that Wilderness himself is an
alter ego of Lowry since the journal tells us that the novel Wilderness is working on is to be called *Dark as the Grave Wherein My
Friend Is Laid*, a novel published posthumously under Lowry's
own name and containing once again a protagonist called Wilderness. In this way, even the identity of Wilderness is questioned.
The narrative of Sigbjørn Wilderness borders on nightmare: "I am
not I. I am Martin Trumbaugh. But I am not Martin Trumbaugh or
perhaps Firmin either, I am a voice" (p. 37). Firmin is, of course,
the central character of Lowry's *Under the Volcano*. We have, once
again, the problem of identifying the narrator, of telling the novelist from the fiction, and perhaps it would be better to call B. S.
Johnson's unnamed narrator just a voice like Lowry's. Yet whereas
Trawl's narrator seems to have an ego but is in search of a past to
explain it, the narrator of "Through the Panama" has a past but is
in search of a stable ego to affix to it. And because of this, the effect
on the journal form in "Through the Panama" is all the more disruptive, throwing into crisis both the dating of the entries and the
status of the text as a discrete physical object.

Like *The Voyage of the Destiny*, "Through the Panama" gives a
definite date to the journal: "Leaving Vancouver, British Colum-
bia, Canada, midnight, November 7, 1947, S.S. *Diderot*, for Rotter-
dam" (p. 26). Subsequent entries are also dated. In *The Voyage of*

the Destiny, I argued that the precise dating of the voyage served to add historical authenticity to the narrative: it denoted a factual accuracy that could be checked by the reader. In "Through the Panama," the initial effect is the same but the stability this seems to offer the reader is quickly undermined both by the problem of the narrator's identity and by a confusion in the dating of entries. The entry following 18 November is marked "*Nov. 19—or 21?*" (p. 36); the following entry is "*Nov. 20—or 21*" (p. 40). This is perhaps not so strange (even given the impossibility that both days might be 21 November) since losing track of the days seems to be a convention of fictive sea journals—only Sir Walter Ralegh of all four narrators keeps an accurate journal and that arguably because, as captain of his ship, it is one of his duties to keep an accurate log of the passage of time. But more disconcerting is the fact that in "Through the Panama" there are two entries for 27 November, one dealing with the ship's passage through the Panama Canal, the other with the following day. Since this discrepancy, which affects an entry central to the narrative, is neither commented upon nor corrected, the gain in authenticity that dating gives is undermined. The discrepancy could be the result of a factual inaccuracy on the part of Wilderness, but it could equally be the result of a fictional freedom to invent on the part of Lowry. The reader has no way of orientating the reading. As Lowry's narrator states: "*Dec. 12. Position Report. S.S. Diderot.* There is no position report" (p. 92). This is in sharp contrast to Sir Walter Ralegh's regular and detailed position reports, and a contrast reinforced by a comparison of the names of their respective ships: *Destiny* gives direction to Ralegh's narrative, *Diderot* at its best serves to underline Wilderness's uncertain status as fiction or nonfiction.

The third way in which the journal form is broken concerns the notion of the journal as a book. I have already pointed out the degree to which *Rites of Passage* and *The Voyage of the Destiny* are seen as physical objects, particularly in respect of the way in which other documents are appended to the manuscript. In *Trawl*, the narrative is thought rather than written so there is no reference to the text as an object, though this does not prevent the inclusion of documents such as a poem or the instructions on a fire-extinguisher (p. 29). "Through the Panama" is again a document, a document the diarist struggles in a storm to keep up: "We stand, bracing ourselves and holding on. This desk thank God is strongly anchored, so I hang on with one hand to desk, write with other. Hope I can read this scrawl later" (p. 93). There is also the framing of other documents within the narrative: poems, newspaper clippings, instructions in French for the abandoning of ship, the questionnaire for the Quarantine and Immigration Officer to be completed by all passengers passing through the Panama Canal.

Yet gradually the documents begin to break free from the journal form. As Martin Trumbaugh (and/or Sigbjørn Wilderness) undergoes a psychological crisis, so annotations from *The Rime of the Ancient Mariner* appear in the margins of the journal: "The Mariner awakes, and his penance begins anew" (p. 38). This is quoted alongside "Martin woke up weeping, however, never before having realized that he had such a passion for the wind and the sunrise." We might like to think of these marginal notes as ironic comments made by Wilderness upon himself. However, since they are not commented upon in the journal entries, their status is open to question. We have no way of knowing whether they are being quoted by Wilderness or Lowry and, thus, whether they are inside the fictive document form (that is, made by Wilderness either at the time or later), or outside (as comments by Lowry on his own fiction). What we have is a collision of texts, the authorship of both being in doubt.

The diary form is also questioned during the actual passage through the Panama Canal since the diary entries are paralleled by a second text to give a typographical representation of the banks of the Canal. From the arrival at the Canal in the evening to lunchtime the following day, the diary entries are paralleled by an early history of the Canal taken, we are told, from Helen Nicolay's *The Bridge of Water* (p. 52).[6] We can initially assume this reworking of Nicolay's book to be written by Wilderness, yet the writerly craft by which it covers two diary entries and then skilfully dovetails back into the journal text is incompatible with the artlessness associated with the diary form—as H. Porter Abbott puts it, the use of the diary strategy has become "a formal attribute of the absence of form" (*Diary Fiction*, p. 19). Though the commentary claims to have been written at the same time, it exceeds the possibilities of the fictive document form and cannot have been written by Wilderness as apparently claimed.

This play between texts is again continued, after lunch, in the Canal, the parallel text being now an alternative commentary on the voyage, drawing a comparison between the Canal and a novel, between the operator of the locks ("who would feel perfectly comfortable if only he did not know that there was yet another man sitting yet higher above him in *his* invisible control tower" [p. 61]) and the novelist. Here, the framing of the diarist by the author

again spirals away into infinity. Yet enough has been said to demonstrate the ways in which "Through the Panama," unlike my
other four journals, breaks down the boundaries of the diary form.
Secondary documents are no longer framed by the diarist's narrative but run parallel to and even themselves frame the diary entries. At the end of "Through the Panama," the form is summed up
in the following: *"The whole is an assembly of apparently incongru-
ous parts, slipping past one another"* (p. 98). And since this comment is both included in and excluded from the text by being placed
in italics—is both a comment by Wilderness yet an echo of Lawrence's description of *Ulysses* quoted earlier in the journal (p. 31)—
it too participates in that slippage.

We have, then, four sea journals, each of which charts a separate
limit of modern diary fiction. *Rites of Passage* returns to the age of
the letter journal to recreate that form for a modern readership. In
Golding, the fictive document is not an imitation of a nonfiction
genre but is more subtly a copy of an imitation, the document doubly
framed, and Edmund Talbot's rationalist discourse is undermined
as much from within as from without, an undermining that leads in
Close Quarters and *Fire Down Below* to an evolution of narrative
form. *The Voyage of the Destiny* stresses the documentary possibilities of the fictive document, using the modern resources of the journal form as a confessional to chart Sir Walter Ralegh's final private
voyage alongside his final public voyage. For Robert Nye, the fictive
document is employed not to invoke a past literary form but to
invoke history. *Trawl* pushes through the literalness of the fictive
document to produce the modern quasi-diary, the diary thought
rather than written. But, more radically, B. S. Johnson's unnamed
narrator throws into doubt the assumed division between fact and
fiction—the quasi-diary is also a quasi-autobiography. "Through
the Panama" adheres more closely to the formal aspect of diary
fiction, but only to disrupt it the more thoroughly. The named narrator is retained but is undermined by being given a number of
alternative names. Lowry, like Golding, is concerned with exploring
the more literary concerns of diary fiction, but does so with a much
more demonic force. The sea journal as fictive document is first
holed by a contradiction of dates and then breaks up as its cargo of
documents shifts and splits its narrative frame. Of all four authors,
Lowry is the most adventurous, and, with the current trend toward
more realist fiction, it is unlikely that many contemporary British

writers will be prepared to risk their own diary fiction in following him.[7]

NOTES

1. For a detailed account of the early sea journal see Lorna Martens, *The Diary Novel*, Chapter 7.

2. My remarks in this section are greatly indebted to Martens, Chapter 8.

3. See Martens, Chapter 10.

4. I am indebted throughout this paragraph to Martens, pp. 133–37.

5. For a fuller examination of this aspect of *Trawl* see Hassam, "True Novel or Autobiography?"

6. It is worth noting that the publication details of Helen Nicolay's book are omitted, thus questioning also its status as a factual document. Only by consulting secondary evidence can the book be established as a genuine document.

7. The British diary novel most similar in form to "Through the Panama" is Ann Quin's *Passages*, half of which is in the form of an annotated diary. However, though *Passages* undermines the diary as a self-contained document, the questioning of the diarist's identity does not extend beyond the frame of the novel (see Chapter 6).

which women traditionally had access. Indeed, as Lorna Martens points out, middle-class women at the turn of the twentieth century were actively encouraged to keep diaries: "The middle-class woman with time on her hands can console and amuse herself by keeping a diary, and confiding in a diary offers a prudent substitute for potentially dangerous confidences made to a friend" (*The Diary Novel*, p. 173). These confidences, presumably, include the treatment of such women by husbands or fathers.

The association of women with diaries is one of the strengths yet also one of the weaknesses of using the diary novel as a means of examining the cultural situation of women. The strength of the domestic diary lies in the presumed accuracy of its record of women's daily experience: it records the activities of individual women, activities that have been marginalized and excluded from what has been termed his-story. As the editor of Hannah Cullwick's diary puts it: "For me, it is precisely her 'ordinariness' that makes Hannah so 'extraordinary.' She is . . . the most thoroughly documented, thoroughly ordinary working-class woman of a period about which we still know all too little" (*The Diaries of Hannah Cullwick*, p. 2). This documentary function of the domestic diary is then transferred to the diary novel, and when the diarist is a woman it is an expectation of the diary novel that this will involve an examination of a women's role in society. Thus, H. Porter Abbott is able to identify certain characteristics specific to the fictive female diarist: "she is a victim of the stereotyping imposed on her by virtue of her gender; her powerlessness is a function of her social condition as a woman" (*Diary Fiction*, p. 16). And as Martens points out, for women writers in Germany around 1900 "the diary form offered a solution for juxtaposing the formulaic with the particular, for showing the impact of formulaic situations and stock catastrophes on a heroine's sensibilities" (p. 176). Given that such criticism of female stereotyping has now become an expectation of the diary novel form, it may be to avoid focussing on feminist concerns that Iris Murdoch uses a male diarist in *The Sea, The Sea*.

On the other hand, the association of women with diaries may also be seen as a weakness. The task of altering the way in which cultural space has been gendered must arguably also involve a realignment of types of discourse; what will be required is a discourse that is not marginalized or is itself a gendered stereotype. According to Sara Lennox, modern women's writing in Germany has most successfully challenged patriarchal discourse "by disrupting traditional literary forms to reveal their suppression of women's voices or by developing new structures of discourse in which female subjects might start to speak themselves" ("Trends in Literary Theory," p. 65). This involves challenging the prevalent model of literary subjectivity in Western culture which is "male: single, unified, teleological" (p. 67). And the fragmentation of such a subjectivity has the additional imperative that "a narrative which takes the form of a series of short, only tenuously connected texts corresponds to the shape of most women's lives, which consist of a series of interruptions" (p. 70). Citing this passage from Lennox, Martens suggests:

One might conjecture that the diary is a particularly attractive form for women's fiction because, as a flexible, open, nonteleological structure, it complements the nonautobiographical quality of women's lives and the traditionally dependent, accommodating female role. A diary can be written in snatches and with little concentration; it is adaptable to the housewife's interrupted day. (*The Diary Novel*, p. 182)

It is unclear whether Martens is being critical here of this association of women with diaries, but it needs to be pointed out that there are degrees of openness and the diary form is not always pushed to the deconstructive lengths that Lennox favours—its traditional flexibility equally favours traditional travel narratives such as the male-gendered sea journal. Moreover, the idea that women write "in snatches and with little concentration" reinforces the idea that what women have to say can be dismissed as white noise, a derogatory idea discussed in Jane Gallop's aptly titled essay, "Snatches of Conversation." I think that while Martens is right in showing how Lennox's comment may apply to women's diary fiction, we should be wary of seeing modern women's diary fiction as necessarily radical. Martens arguably is trying to mitigate the weakness of the domestic diary as a gendered discourse by stressing its strength as a record of women's experience, yet the two need to be distinguished: we might merely be dealing with a traditional association of the diary as a flexible form with, in Martens' own words, a "traditionally dependent, accommodating female role."

What I want to suggest, therefore, is that we can analyze modern women's diary fiction according to two differing strategies by which the diary novel might examine the cultural role of women. The first is what we might call the documentary mode, the way in which women diarists examine their experience of cultural stereotyping and the way in which women are restricted by the physical, if culturally gendered, domestic space allotted them. Such a strategy can be aligned with what Mary Jacobus sees as an Anglo-American and empiricist feminist reading, the assumption of which "is of an unbroken continuity between 'life' and 'text'—a mimetic relation whereby women's writing, reading, or culture, instead of being produced, reflect a knowable reality" ("Is There a Woman," p. 138). Here the diary is an accurate record of women's experience in the real world.

The second strategy focusses on the means by which women might attain freedom from patriarchal discourse through writing, through questioning the way in which the diary itself rather than physical space is gendered. The alignment here is with Jacobus' description of French feminist criticism:

> . . . the French insistence on écriture féminine—on woman as a writing-effect instead of an origin—asserts not the sexuality of the text but the textuality of sex. Gender difference, produced, not innate, becomes a matter of the structuring of a genderless libido in and through patriarchal discourse. Language itself would at once repress multiplicity and heterogeneity—true difference—by the tyranny of hierarchical oppositions (man/woman) and simultaneously work to overthrow that tyranny by interrogating the limits of meaning. (p. 138)

In what I will call the discursive mode, then, the female diarist challenges the form of the diary as a vehicle for adequately transcribing women's experience and seeks a new definition of reality "by interrogating the limits of meaning." These are, it should be pointed out, differing emphases rather than mutually exclusive strategies, but at the risk of overschematizing, it may be that while the prevalence of the documentary mode tends toward a reluctant acceptance of a lack of freedom, the discursive mode tends towards a mystical escape through a nonreferential use of language. The usefulness of such a poetics will be judged by its results.

Eva Figes' *Nelly's Version* and Jane Rogers' *The Ice Is Singing* are both diaries by women attempting to escape from domestic incarceration. In this sense they are primarily documentary records of women's experience. However, neither is restricted to the documentary mode, and in both novels keeping a diary not only traces the parabola of escape and return but is an attempt to articulate the discursive condition of their incarceration. Not only does writing a diary involve an engagement with writing in the way that the diary strategy often does by virtue of its concern with Prince's "theme of writing a diary" ("The Diary Novel," p. 479); it also involves an engagement specifically with discourse, the way in which incarceration and freedom in women's lives can be related to language and narrative.

The Ice Is Singing is comfortably accommodated as diary fiction. It comprises a series of diary entries kept by a named narrator, Marion, over the five-week period of Sunday 2 February 1986 to Saturday 8 March, and this specificity of narrator and dating is matched by a specificity of place, the narrator spending the time driving through the snow-covered landscape of the Pennines between Barnsley and Manchester. However, a textual note tells us that Jane Rogers wrote part of the novel while Writer in Residence at Northern College, Barnsley, in 1985–86. There is, therefore, despite the specificity of the work and the coincidence of time and place with the background of composition, a very clear fictional frame, and the discussion of the nature of fiction is self-contained on the level of the story.

Nelly's Version is similarly novelistic, though by contrast it employs the more common novelistic convention of omitting the date of the diary and the place in which the action occurs. This strategy of omission is naturalized in the story by being attributed to the diarist's amnesia. Yet while the diarist's failure to discover the date is somewhat contrived (it depends solely on the chance concealment of the date on a newspaper), her failure to discover where she is becomes part of a more general theme, that of the loss of meaning of social and linguistic sign systems: "I looked at the station frontage and saw for the first time that it had a name, though it was meaningless and recalled nothing" (p. 50). Other attempts similarly founder:

A railway timetable on one wall was almost illegible in the gloom, and anyhow I found the numerous columns of numbers and names impossible to decipher: I did not know at what point to start looking, or how to go on from here. (p. 51)

"Where does it go . . . the up train?" I asked, feeling somewhat foolish, and more so when he [the porter] answered, banging his hand trolley about in a dark doorway: "Depends where you want to go, doesn't it? It'll take you anywhere, provided you know when to get off and change. It's all a matter of connections." (p. 52)

The problem for the diarist in *Nelly's Version* is precisely that she has metaphorically got off and changed, has escaped from all the family and domestic ties that entrap her as a woman; but the condition of her escape, her amnesia, prohibits her from making the connections necessary to find an alternative destination. Having rejected gender stereotyping, she lacks an alternative discourse.

The opening of *The Ice Is Singing* employs a similar metaphor to that of *Nelly's Version*, though in this case the diarist attempts to transcend a stream of cars rather than a train ride. Marion, leaving home, drives out onto a motorway and gets caught up in the traffic:

There were a lot of cars. It took me by surprise. Moving very fast. They swerve in and out. Or stop, or turn. As if they know exactly where they're going. . . .

I thought it would be best to stop. It was not possible to reach the side because they were passing on my left and right. I stopped in the middle, switching on the hazard-lights. The stream of cars divided easily around me and flowed on. (p. 1)

Having herself been left by a husband and teenage daughters who seem to know exactly where they are going, Marion abandons the crush of her own life to search for an ungendered breathing space among the snow-covered hills of the Pennines: "My head is full of emptiness, a white eggshell. I drive in silence to keep it so. . . . I move to keep blank (it works); driving all day with a ball of thoughts and feelings rolling along behind me, ready to crush, a carelessly chucked giant's marble" (p. 2). Yet having created this emotional blankness Marion still feels drawn to fill the blankness by diary writing, by filling a diary with comforting stories made up out of her own muddled life: "She names the pain. She identifies it, telling herself that thus it can be remedied, later in the story. Suggesting to herself—comforting herself—deluding herself again— that things follow on, make sense, have remedies" (p. 15). What Marion comes to realize is that the process of fictionalizing her life—the story-telling and the "naming"—is an evasion of the chaos of her life, an evasion of the chaos of the ordinary life:

There is nothing to resolve. Nothing so concrete. Just images, some familiar, some forgotten. Just times, moods, impressions. An undigested life— a ragbag. It's all ordinary enough. . . .

OK. I've stopped. I'm not running. I'm not hiding. I'm not . . . in someone else's story, I'm in my life, and there won't be a resolution. There isn't the structure for it. It's not a story, it's a list of days.

All right. Make a list. It is after all the most sensible, housewifely thing to do. Make a list, tidy up. You can at least manage that, if not to resolve. (p. 57)

Marion falls back on the list, the discursive form more appropriate to the ordinary everyday life of the housewife than the controlled and ordered narrative of the short story. Yet Marion rejects even this: "Unless it is complete the list is a distortion, and the only way to complete it would be to write continuously" (p. 145). At the end of *The Ice Is Singing*, therefore, Marion abandons diary keeping because both stories and lists tidy up life: "I am returning because I am not a story. There is no controlled shape—beyond the circle my journey away and back will describe. That is a freedom. My life goes on, shapelessly, raggedly, from day to day. I don't know what will happen. But my life goes on" (p. 153). Marion passes beyond the diary as a record of women's experience into a discursive silence and a stoical acceptance of the meaninglessness of life.

I have traced the argument of *The Ice Is Singing* in some detail because it demonstrates the problem women writers face in trying to combine both the documentary mode and the discursive mode. In what I have called the documentary mode, *The Ice Is Singing* is an accurate portrayal of Marion's emotional experience as a woman caught up in a world in which she has lost her identity: "In the mirror I see a woman I've never met, with tiny squinting eyes and swollen bleeding lips" (p. 17). The diary is used to reflect the incoherence of women's lives when gauged against a traditional totalizing and, as argued above by Lennox, masculine teleology. Yet looked at in the discursive mode, this referential function relies on the falsity of a gendered discourse, the way in which language, like the list, always imposes categories on experience. Marion also wants to reject the constitutive function of language. The problem for Marion, in short, is how to write about women's experience without categorizing it.

The Ice Is Singing is, therefore, a novel about how to transcribe women's experience, a transcription that succeeds in the documentary mode but fails when confronted by the discursive mode, the possibility of rewriting the life. As a documentary novel, *The Ice Is Singing* does indeed have a "controlled shape" beyond the circle of Marion's journey, and if that shape is not merely the story it is nonetheless a narrative about women's experience, a way of relating the events that logically leads to the outcome. Yet by adopting the B. S. Johnson argument that "telling stories is telling lies" ("how neat, and satisfying, and necessary are the lies of fiction" [p. 147]), Marion is forced to push beyond the list and the fragmentary narrative of the diary to renounce all forms of writing because writing is always meaningful, a distortion of the meaninglessness of life—"Little things . . . resist explanation. They won't stand still to have metaphors hung round their necks like mayoral chains" (p. 15). Marion must stop writing, a strategy that allows the diary as novel to retain a controlled shape and "mayoral" metaphors since ultimately the novel represents what is rejected. Like B. S. Johnson's *Albert Angelo*, *The Ice Is Singing* is a narrative about the inadequacy of narrative.

In contrast to *The Ice Is Singing*, Eva Figes' *Nelly's Version* questions the relationship between narrative and the form of women's lives not by abandoning writing but by leaving unresolved certain discursive contradictions within the work. The opening lines of the novel establish the connected themes of naming (the creation of identity through naming) and of narrative form (in this case popular cinema): "He watched my hand slide across the page as I signed a false name and address in the hotel register. I admired my own coolness: I had seen it done in so many films and now I was doing it myself" (p. 9). Like Marion in *The Ice Is Singing*, Nelly Dean has fled from incarceration in a gendered domestic space to take refuge in a hotel and, again like Marion, to take refuge in an emotional blankness, in this case the result of amnesia. Yet while Marion is first drawn into a world of discourse only to find a certain freedom by rejecting it, Nelly Dean remains caught in a double-bind—existing discursive structures inevitably imprison a woman, yet life cannot go on without them.

Once inside her hotel room Nelly finds she has in her suitcase bundles of banknotes and a minimal wardrobe "more suitable for a wet weekend than any sort of great adventure imaginable" (p. 17). She plans, therefore, to use the money to scrap her previous identity "once I had decided who I was, and what rôle I was supposed to be playing" (p. 17). However, deciding who she is and what she should do presents her with a problem: the condition of her escape, her amnesia, though it gives her the theoretical freedom to invent a persona, also robs her of any fixed point by which to stabilize a persona. Without knowing where she is or even what day it is, she finds herself remaining like the river running past the hotel in a state of flux: "I did not know its name. But could it, anyhow, be right to name a river, which was liquid in continuous motion, and could not really be called the same river for two minutes together?" (p. 28). In other words, remaining like the river may be the ideal, but at the same time she finds that "total freedom can become an intolerable weight pressing on one's shoulders" (p. 32). Life may be unshaped, therefore, but lack of shape gives the individual no control; and so after an unsettling dream Nelly decides to keep a diary: "I have decided that, if I cannot control my sleeping hours, I must at least try to establish a workable shape and pattern in my waking ones. To that end, I have begun to keep a systematic record in my new notebook" (p. 67). As she puts it later: "Everybody should have a story which is coherent, with a certain consistency" (p. 187).

The problem with this position, however, is that Nelly discovers that a stable identity can only be established by succumbing to preexisting models. Even to book into a hotel room she has had to adopt two roles, the first that inferred by naming (Nelly Dean), the second by having to invent a husband who will arrive later with her luggage: "my arrival, unaccompanied and without prior booking, ceased to be questionable the moment I ceased being just myself, by myself, and became a married woman in the looming protective shadow of a mythical husband who would shortly arrive to join her" (p. 10). The only workable shape is an intersubjective shape, a shape that is in these terms fictive both by being an imaginative construct and by its reliance on fictional models—Nelly Dean is that model of Martens' "accommodating female" represented in Emily Brontë's *Wuthering Heights*, a domestic servant whose function is merely to enable someone else's tale to be told. And Nelly's reiterated feeling that she is in a play "waiting for a cue of some sort" (p. 25) is reinforced by the antirealism of her discovering various versions of *Nelly's Version* in the local library. Gradually, therefore, Nelly finds herself compelled to accept the inevitability of socially prescribed roles, of female stereotypes that have already been given the consistency of characters out of novels or plays. She is forced to play the role of mother and grandmother by the simple act of being labeled a mother by a stranger who insists she is his son—"human logic as a net of meridians and parallels thrown across the universe to make it captive" (p. 118)—and Nelly finally allows herself to be incarcerated once again as "the price I have had to pay for the tattered remnants of freedom" (p. 186).

Compared with *The Ice Is Singing*, *Nelly's Version* is a pessimistic work, though in tone the two novels have surprisingly similar endings:

I am not returning home because it will be spring and my heart and sorrows have melted with the snows. The poor battered land shows no signs of spring, encourages no such thought. . . .

I am returning because I am not a story. . . . My life goes on, shapelessly, raggedly, from day to day. I don't know what will happen. But my
life goes on. (*The Ice Is Singing*, p. 153)

It gets dark early now, and the shadows lengthen across the lawn by mid-
afternoon, even before I have had my tea. Dark evenings lie ahead, and
the long cold nights. I do not know where I shall go from here. (*Nelly's
Version*, p. 218)

Both novels use nature imagery to invoke a bleak atmosphere, and
both end with an uncertainty about the future. Yet while in *The Ice
Is Singing* Marion manages to achieve a limited freedom ("life goes
on"), the best Nelly can hope for is a second escape, an escape that
will lead her back to the beginning of the novel and a second inevitable failure. In other words, Marion can escape by abandoning
fiction and thus also her diary. On the other hand, for Nelly, being
part of a fiction is a condition of life, a condition that, in a world
where the prevailing gender models deny women freedom, denies
Nelly an escape. Nelly fails to find a discursive freedom.

The problem, however, of summarizing the two novels in this
way is that it suggests that, as novels, *The Ice Is Singing* is more
successful than *Nelly's Version* in escaping from the confines of a
male discourse. Yet if we accept that, as Lennox puts it, "The model
for literary subjectivity in Western culture is male: single, unified,
teleological" ("Trends in Literary Theory," p. 67), although *The Ice
Is Singing* argues against such a subjectivity, it does so in a novel
that retains a certain teleology and integration. Lennox is refer-
ring specifically to female autobiography, and, if we take the case
of the diary in the novel, Marion's diary offers the reader the stability of a single subject: although the novel argues against a unified
subjectivity by paralleling diary and short stories, the short stories
are comfortably contained by the diary sections in the way that the
diary is contained by the novel. On the other hand, in *Nelly's Version* the discrete boundary between novel and diary is undermined
from within, and, though the novel as a whole can be attributed to
Eva Figes, Nelly's diary exceeds a discrete subjectivity: nowhere
does Nelly acknowledge the source of her false name in Emily
Brontë's *Wuthering Heights*, and neither does she draw attention
to the parallel between the man in her attic whom she tries to force
out by setting fire to her house (and who it appears is her husband)
and the "mad woman in the attic" in the novel by Charlotte Brontë,
Jane Eyre. More radically, the old woman whom Nelly first sees

reflected in a mirror coming to lunch in the hotel ("the epitome of all old ladies of stage and screen" [p. 22]) becomes both Nelly's next door neighbour and finally Nelly herself, the hotel becoming the convalescent home. By the use of such parallels both inside and outside Nelly's diary, *Nelly's Version* suggests that it may be possible to find a certain freedom within discourse by reworking rather than abandoning stereotypes, and though Nelly herself is once again incarcerated the novel itself does, through the establishment of areas of indeterminacy, more seriously challenge a closed, unified, and teleological structure. Nelly's attempts to rewrite a reality more appropriate to a woman, even if ultimately unsuccessful, involve both a questioning of realism and an undermining of the position of the diary in the novel which goes beyond the form of *The Ice Is Singing*. As a diary *Nelly's Version* succeeds as documentary, as a novel it succeeds as discourse.

In *Nelly's Version* and *The Ice Is Singing* both diarists use writing a diary to examine the life from which they have managed to escape, the emotional and intellectual constrictions placed on them as wives and mothers that result in their bids to be free. In each case these bids for freedom are associated with a form of mental breakdown. In Emma Tennant's *The Bad Sister* and in Ann Quin's *Three,* both diarists again suffer a breakdown and again this breakdown coincides with a need to escape. Yet the diary in both Tennant and Quin is used less to investigate a lack of freedom than as a means of locating a deeper reality and a lasting, if not totally unqualified, freedom. In particular, this search for a deeper, freer reality involves in the writing of the diary an entry into fantasy, the creation of a fantasy discourse that is contrasted in the novels themselves with a discourse that is not only rationalist but also specifically masculine.

In Tennant's *The Bad Sister*, "The Journal of Jane Wild" is sandwiched between an "Editor's Narrative" and an "Editor's Note." This is a traditional pseudo-nonfiction technique, an editorial note functioning to supply background information and relate how the diary came to be published. However, since it is now acceptable for fictive diaries to be published as novels without the need for an editorial introduction, as in *Nelly's Version*, we have to be careful not to see it as simply a supplement but as part of the overall strategy of the novel itself. Specifically, in *The Bad Sister*, although the editor is unnamed, it is clear that the editor is a man and this man as a journalist is trying to solve the mystery of the deaths of the financier Michael Dalzell and his daughter Ishbel. As part of his investigations, he discovers the journal of Jane Wild, Dalzell's illegitimate daughter, who disappeared after the killings and whom he eventually becomes convinced carried out the murders. Of importance to the form of the novel, however, is that this man presents to the reader as part of his evidence other documents, letters from Dalzell's acquaintances, newspaper clippings, and a psychiatrist's report on Jane's journal, as well as the journal itself. Jane's journal is contrasted with a number of documents all of which represent aspects of a predominantly masculine, rationalist discourse. The novel offers the diary of Jane Wild not only as documentary evidence but as an alternative feminine discourse that challenges the documentary parameters of the editorial frame.

This aspect contrasts with Tennant's model for the form of *The Bad Sister*, James Hogg's *The Private Memoirs and Confessions of a Justified Sinner* (1824). In Hogg there is again the editorial frame and again reference to the documentary testament of others. However, the memoir of the justified sinner himself, Robert Wringhim, is itself a similar documentary attempt to record and preserve for a public and specifically Christian audience what has occurred, even to the extent of printing the greater part of his confession. The editorial narrative and Wringhim's narrative differ in the kind of evidence they offer, but both are masculine, rationalist, officially endorsed types of discourse. By making Hogg's "sinner" female, Tennant calls attention to the relationship between discourse and women.

The action of Jane Wild's diary takes place over five days, beginning with her return home from a party on a Saturday night and ending with her slipping away from a second party on the following Thursday night. There are also indications in the diary that the action is set some time around 1977 (p. 53) and in London (p. 45). Yet the function of these references is, like the editorial documentation, to establish a reality and a realist discourse from which sections of Jane's diary can depart.

After her return from the first party Jane undergoes a form of metamorphosis, not simply by hacking off her hair in front of the bathroom mirror, but by a process of actual anatomical change:

I went back to the bathroom and re-examined my appearance. Women and mirrors; mirrors and women. My face seemed to have grown much smaller and my eyes were round and rimmed with exhaustion, black as the underside of a moth. (p. 36)

Jane's experience here owes less to Hogg's justified sinner who retains his own mortal shape throughout than to Robert Louis Stevenson's Dr. Jekyll for a whom a loss of stature and an unspecifiable deformity accompanies his transformation into the pure evil of his bad brother, Edward Hyde. However, while Dr Jekyll steps out of an identity in which good and evil coexist, Jane Wild sheds a simple sexual identity for something more complex. Following the change in her facial structure Jane discovers that someone has placed at the foot of her bed a pair of jeans and a denim jacket: "I looked down at my body before I pulled off the silk party dress. My breasts were tiny now, and the bra that had once contained them looked large and empty. Like a shroud, I thought, as I stood there paralysed a moment, unable to move" (p. 36). Jane steps out of her identity as a woman, or rather, the biological female sexually exploited by Tony, the man she lives with, and that female who shares sexual identity with the other women of her street, the women of the hostel for battered women and the women who frequent the lesbian nightclub next door. Yet in her new form, "in my perfect androgyny" (p. 39), she represents something not separate from men but something that transcends the difference, "a new genetic pattern like a neon sign in cuneiform, something ancient and known and at the same time infinitely strange" (p. 37). And in this new form Jane comes to the edge of a new world: "I arrive at the port. So this is where I will disembark for another world! . . . I pull the gun from my pocket and make my way along the right hand tentacle of the harbour" (p. 39). Jane kills one of the sailors she meets in a bar in the harbour, a figure whom we assume represents her father, but she is not to earn her freedom until the end of the diary when in another fantasy world she kills again, this time her half-sister Ishbel and the one who represents the "Bad Sister" of the novel's title. In so doing she steps into her own death.

It is not necessary here to go into Jane's relationship to the witchlike Meg who gives Jane the power to enter this fantasy world, though it is worth mentioning that Meg's powers can be seen as the feminine counterpart to the rationalist scientific and specifically masculine powers of Dr. Jekyll. And certainly the figure of Gilmartin, from whom Meg may have derived some of her powers, is far more sexually ambivalent than Hogg's Gil-martin, being something of a male muse, as Tennant herself has said (Haffenden, *Novelists in Interview*, p. 292). However, enough has been said to demonstrate the kind of questions *The Bad Sister* examines. As the editor puts it:

Is she a victim of the modern resurgence of the desire for the old magic of
wholeness, for unified sensibilities? Is she really an example, as some
women would have it now, of the inherent "splitness" of women, a condition passed on from divided mother to divided daughter until such day as
they regain their vanished power? (p. 137)

The editor also draws attention to the political dimension of the
death of the wealthy, capitalist father: "I can only marvel at the
cleverness of Margaret, or Meg, who appears, to borrow the words
of a friend of mine to whom I recently showed the journal, to have
'used Freud and Jung to achieve the aims of Marx'" (p. 137). What
is of importance here is the way in which Jane's diary raises these
questions yet at the same time is not reducible to a demonstration
of any one of them in the way that Stevenson's Dr Jekyll or even
Hogg's Robert Wringhim is able to reflect upon his *alter ego* and
the relationship between good and evil. In *The Bad Sister* the distinction between the good and the bad is more problematic, Jane's
victim's are less morally good than Wringhim's, and clearly Jane
Wild is writing neither a medical casebook nor a Christian confessional. In other words, the editorial discourse enacts the kind of
masculine rationalism that Jane's diary as an irrational fantasy is
set on subverting. In particular, the diary form itself moves beyond
the diary convention, and there is only a single reference to the
writing of the diary: "I write this as the hour draws near" (p. 120).
At other times the diary form moves into the "quasi-diary" form
of B. S. Johnson's *Trawl*, becoming a present-tense narration of
events as they occur: "There is a wind blowing today, the air in the
street is milky white, and scraps of white paper float along at first
floor level. . . . I walk up to Notting Hill Gate. . . . The flowers in the
sloping gardens are smothered with fine white dust" (p. 45). And
since this style is used to describe Jane's final escape beyond reality, the diary finally abandons altogether the stable point necessary for its writing.

Ann Quin's *Three* is a similar work in that it contrasts the diary of
a woman with other types of discourse. After undergoing an abor-
tion, "S" (she remains an initial throughout the novel) comes to live
with a childless couple, Ruth and Leonard, but goes missing after
six months and is presumed by the police to have committed suicide. However, among her possessions are some written diaries and
taperecordings, and these two voices of the girl alternate with a
third-person narrative in which the couple find it increasingly dif-

ficult to sustain their insularity from the world outside. In addition, parts of the diaries of Ruth and Leonard are reproduced within the third-person sections.

Leonard's diary is unemotional, a record of events:

October 15th	Clear day. Sun at last. S hasn't returned.
October 16th	Rain again. Still no sign of S. Informed police.
October 18th	Boat found capsized. Coat identified. Also note in pocket —looks like suicide.
October 19th	Two hours questioning by police sergeant. River and coastline dragged.
October 20th	R in bed all day. Translation completed.
October 21st	Dinner with the Blakeleys. A good hock.
October 22nd	Orchids making progress especially Barbatum. (p. 41)

This *journal externe* is the discourse of masculine efficiency, the disappearance of S apparently having no effect on Leonard's work as a translator or his ability to enjoy a dinner party with friends. In this diary Leonard marks with a black cross those days on which he has sex with his wife Ruth, much to her disgust: "Oh no Leon really why in heaven's name how horrid putting things like that down. No more than your temperature chart love same thing in a way. Not at all it's rather nasty what you do besides mine's purely for medical reasons. And mine?" (p. 42). Sex for Leonard has become a matter of clinical routine, like his diary, without emotion. Leonard admits feelings only for his collection of rare orchids whose phallic "Turrets of intense purple" (p. 12) symbolize "the purple tip" (p. 44) of his own sexuality. Yet in a taperecording Leonard admits that this male efficiency is only a way of controlling contradictions within himself: "Three aspects yes yes that can be recognised. Now. The boy. Youth. Man. Each contradicting. How to come to terms? A compromise" (p. 120). None of these roles is self-sufficient, and even though he can contrast himself as the practical husband "Known for action alone" with a younger self "playing with real lives to create a bigger and better world where all things everybody would be equal," that idealism was "a game you–he watched played out against a background of subterfuge. Violence. Torture. Never witnessed. Only whispered about behind locked doors" (p. 120).

Ruth's diary is more in the tradition of the *journal intime*, an examination of feelings and sensibility rather than a record of events: "If only we had a child. Does he wish this as much? Would it make me feel any different basically? The response is no longer there. This much I know. He is concerned only with achieving his own orgasm and I refuse absolutely to be exploited that way" (p. 124). And like Leonard in his taped diary, her present loss of identity leads Ruth to reconsider her past:

When we met he was a God, a brother I never had, perhaps a father too. His faults were endearing. I felt I understood. In awe of his idealism, intelligence, and above all secure in his respect for me. When did all that falter, what day, night did I feel this appalling separation, a certain loss of identity? (p. 124)

What both Ruth and Leonard are being forced to reassess is the complementary stereotypes of male and female, the strong husband and the accommodating wife, and a consequent loss of mutual self-definition through their sexual relationship. This leads to a turning in upon their own sexuality, Leonard with his phallic orchids, Ruth's narcissism being expressed by undressing before a mirror: "She ... opened an ornamental box, tried on jewellery. Bracelets slipped up her arms. ... She put them on her ankles. Undid her dress, put a dozen necklaces on, some draped over her breasts. In front of the mirror she pulled her breasts up by holding several necklaces above her neck" (p. 12). The result of this narcissism is that both characters merely have their loss of identity reflected back at themselves, a regressive loss of center symbolized by Leonard's reflection of himself in the mirrors over a pub bar: "mirrors reflected other mirrors, gave three images of himself, each dwindled" (p. 121).

Throughout *Three* both Ruth and Leonard remain locked out of each other and locked into a closed circuit of self-reflection. And yet the drama of the novel depends on them being forced to recognize the sterility of this situation (symbolically the two are childless) by their "adoption" of the third party of the novel's title. This drama depends on the diary strategy in two ways. To begin with, S has already passed out of their lives at the start of the novel, and it is the discovery of S's diaries that prompts both Ruth and Leonard to take up similar projects of self-scrutiny, Leonard complementing his written diary by a taperecording after listening to S's recordings (p. 52), and Ruth taking up diary writing as a new practice, not apparently having kept a diary before (p. 61). This new type of introspection may also represent another aspect of their individual narcissism, but their diary keeping does make possible the finding and reading of each other's diary, and a recognition of the other's point of view.

The second way in which the drama of the novel depends upon the diary strategy is by the temporal intercutting of the narrative of S's stay with Ruth and Leonard (told through S's diaries) with the third-person narrative dealing with the lives of Ruth and Leonard immediately after S's disappearance. In *The Bad Sister*, the diary is in its entirety framed by an editorial narrative, but in *Three* the strategy of intercutting the diary narrative with the narrative of those characters who read it allows such fictive readers a more important place in the novel than that of an editor; it also more fully dramatizes the effect of their reading. In other words, the reader of *Three* is presented with S's assessment of Ruth and Leonard at the same point in the narrative as such revelations are presented to Ruth and Leonard themselves.

S's narrative itself has two forms, a written diary and a taperecording which covers roughly the same period and which, because it is printed as part of the novel, also functions as a type of diary. Two sections of both the diary and the taperecording alternate with the third-person narrative to give *Three* eight narrative sections in all and make half the novel the narrative of S. The relationship between all three types of discourse is complex, a complexity that parallels that between the characters themselves and which requires a more detailed discussion than there is room for here. But certain generalizations can be made.

Once the reader has become used to the style of the third-person narrative, particularly the lack of punctuation in direct speech, it becomes relatively easy to read and provides much of the background information to the diary sections. Its referentiality provides the structure of events, the story element of the narrative. In contrast, the taped sections are, as Ruth points out, "difficult to follow the way she says things" (p. 51). The problem here is that the way the tapes are typographically represented on the pages together with a poetic syntax and imagery make a referential narrative hard to recover:

Dreams. Day dreams
fashioned
from white walls. His thoughts. Female semen seep
through undergrowth. (p. 38)

The tapes, indeed both of S's narratives, incorporate a high degree of self-referentiality:

> . . . Incidents dwelt on
> imagination
> dictates its own vocabulary.
> Clarity
> confusion. (p. 20)

There is both clarity of image and a confusion of a recoverable meaning, though some incidents are recognizable and recur in the written diary sections. What these tapes seem to represent is a half-conscious attempt by S to verbalize certain memories and sexual fantasies, allowing the imagination, as a form of therapy, to dictate its own vocabulary. In other words, the taped sections are largely an imaginative investigation of S's memory, particularly as it reflects on her childhood, her father's desertion of her mother, and the house full of her father's female relatives in which she was brought up: "A place that becomes / another place. Defeats time. Contradicts / movements / gives dimensions" (p. 101).

S's written diaries are somewhere between the stifling and referential world of Ruth and Leonard and the poetic world of the tapes. Though the style is the most conventional of all three narrative styles used in *Three* and the diary is clearly a record of actual events, the construction of S's written diary undermines a clear narrative progression in a number of ways. First, the diary entries are themselves variously headed—"March," "Mid-week," "Saturday"—a strategy that at once suggests an intersubjective framework and at the same time denies it. Second, the diary does not progress by a novelistic connecting of events, the diary entries remaining, as is expected of a nonfiction diary, discrete and unconnected narratives. And third, there remains the element of fantasy that occurs both in a record of sexual fantasies shared with a former lover (who may or may not be Leonard) and in the abstract comments or imaginative dimension of the real: "Patterns reshaped in a form already designed shall anticipate all alternatives, become a measure of a certain consistency. The space between is no less significant than the place occupied at the time" (p. 53). The taped and the written diary sections of *Three*, therefore, contrast with the third-person narrative by combining to produce not a realist discourse but the diary as an open structure which itself questions realism: "Confronted by words, names, dates. A jigsaw, secretly known off by heart, but tossed about, making it harder to piece together—which piece fits in precisely where?" (p. 69). Like Jane Wild in *The Bad Sister*, S uses fantasy to pass beyond the limits of the real: "I long to wade in up to the very limits of imagination if possible. Gain another level, an added dimension" (p. 62).

The use of the word "wade" here is a semantic play on the way in which S gains that added dimension by going missing while out boating, and it is worth tracing the significance of S's death in terms of escape. The house by the sea is overlooked by the Sugarloaf mountain, at the base of which is a lake. Both mountain and lake have a symbolic meaning, S having to climb the mountain in order to escape the past, the house she was brought up in: "The mountain. Sometimes seen / that has to be climbed. / Pursued / by fantasies / fears / memory / by that other place. / The house / at the top / of the avenue" (p. 27). Significantly the trip to the lake and the mountain planned by all three is called off due to drizzle: "The lake / in the middle / of the mountains. Isn't marked on the map. We'll go up there perhaps tomorrow. They say. Oh dear it would rain. She says. Going back to play patience. He with orchids" (p. 104). It is typical of Ruth and Leonard that they fail to grasp opportunities to escape from their stultifying domesticity and narcissism: "The possibility of what might have been sinks away. Into what is left" (p. 115). Yet S herself remains determined to get to the lake: "If I closed my eyes I could see the lake. . . . I knew it could be touched, and would not be fragmented by my touch" (p. 143). It is by this lake that the police eventually find a body, and though a definite connection is not made, it is clearly probable that this "unidentified young woman" (p. 131) is S. Moreover, this unidentified young woman has not drowned but has been murdered by an angler's knife and a hammer.

S, then, finally escapes by an acceptance of violence, an acceptance of that "background of subterfuge. Violence. Torture" (p. 120) part recognized by Leonard and domesticated by both he and Ruth through such devices as a pistol-shaped cigarette lighter (p. 10) and their use of the swimming pool: the pool acts as a substitute for the nearby sea and (drained) as a mock theatre where, together with S, they enact masked mime shows. Indeed, the invasion of one of these mime shows by outsiders from the beach (p. 136) is doubly predictive of the ending of *Three*, both as a figure of the underlying violence and because the intruders seem to be involved in S's death. The inference is that S has been killed in a sexual ritual by the invaders from the beach: "Yesterday evening when rowing past the breakwater, I recognised several of the men who had beaten up L. They played some game with knives on the sand, and beckoned me over" (p. 139). Disturbingly, an entry in S's diary suggests that this ritual has, like the mime shows, been organized by S herself: "After all I have become the victim now, and from that there is no turning back" (p. 135). Yet both Ruth and Leonard are implicated in the violence by their failure to break out of their two-dimensional relationship: "Narrow dimensions of theirs catch me up into an appalling lethargy, when anything would be welcome as a release. They swing each other against walls that bounce them back into themselves" (p. 72). Whether or not S's death will shock the couple out of their domesticity is left open, the third-person narrative not continuing beyond Leonard reading of the discovery of the body in a newspaper report. However, the ending of S's final narrative suggests it will not: "The boat is ready, as planned. All that's necessary now is a note. I know nothing will change" (p. 143).

In *Three*, then, as in *The Bad Sister*, the diary of a woman traces the movement away from a sexual relationship that cannot transcend the divisions of social stereotyping. In both cases, too, the escape is from the rigidity of sexual difference. In *The Bad Sister*, the editor remarks of the body supposed to be that of Jane Wild that "There was no way . . . in which it was possible to tell the sex of the corpse. There was something completely hermaphroditic about it" (p. 140), a contrast to the body of Hogg's Robert Wringhim which remains male. In *Three*, this escape from sexual difference is inferred through one of S's sexual fantasies ("Dual roles / realised. Yes yes / yes / Be a boy. If you like. Anything. Be / Just be" [p. 114]) and by her taking all the different mime-show masks with her (p. 45). In life and as women, both Jane Wild and S are victims, and the residue of the death this disturbingly involves for both diarists is a discourse that itself suggests that a new type of diary writing, one that is contrasted in the novels with a masculine, rationalist realism, is necessary to match this freedom. In *Three* and in *The Bad Sister*, the documentary mode is associated with male narrators, and its rejection in favour of the discursive mode allows the diary to become an accomplice to the woman's freedom rather than to remain, as in *The Ice Is Singing* and in *Nelly's Version*, dependent on stereotypes and a barrier to freedom. The reality of being a woman necessarily entails a new type of writing, one that must break with a patriarchal realism.

I have outlined, above, two differing strategies by which women writers have used the diary novel to investigate gender issues. In Rogers and Figes, the emphasis is on documenting or exposing the repressive nature of a culturally gendered domesticity. To this extent, while both Rogers and Figes suggest a collusion between cultural stereotypes and literary representation, neither diarist moves beyond the documentary mode necessary to represent social conditions. In Tennant and Quin, however, representation is itself challenged by the diarists themselves, and diary writing becomes a fantasy discourse that, the novels suggest, enables women to transcend the limitations of a masculine realism. To the degree that the diarist herself in Doris Lessing's *The Golden Notebook* tries to become a "free woman" through first the one and then the other mode, I shall look at *The Golden Notebook* in terms of how it assesses their relative merits and implications as feminist textual strategies.

The most obvious way in which *The Golden Notebook* examines the relationship of the diary to reality is by having the protagonist, Anna Wulf, keep four separate records of her day-to-day life: "I keep four notebooks, a black notebook, which is to do with Anna Wulf the writer, a red notebook, concerned with politics; a yellow notebook, in which I make stories out of my experience; and a blue notebook which tries to be a diary" (pp. 461–62). These notebooks reflect the fact that "Human beings are so divided, are becoming more and more divided, *and more subdivided in themselves*" (p. 79; Lessing's italics). In keeping these four notebooks, Anna has, as the unidentified editor puts it, "almost automatically, divided herself into four, and then, from the nature of what she had written, named these divisions" (p. 75).

There are three main movements in the diary form of the Blue Notebook, the notebook that "tries to be a diary," and these trace the argument of *The Golden Notebook* as a whole. The first movement concerns those entries that immediately follow Anna's decision to keep a diary: "Why don't I keep a diary? Obviously, my changing everything into fiction is simply a means of concealing something from myself" (p. 232). Anna here is trying to avoid the falsification of her experience by turning it into stories; as she says of her first novel, *Frontiers of War*: "why did I not write an account of what had happened instead of shaping a 'story.' . . . Why a story at all—not that it was a bad story, or untrue, or that it debased anything. Why not, simply, the truth?" (pp. 81–82). The problem seems to be that while the narrative may be factually true, its analysis of events or the meaning it carries through its narrative structure is not "the truth." This position is similar to that of Jane Rogers's *The Ice Is Singing*, which clearly owes a large debt to Doris Lessing; the intention behind diary keeping in both cases is to avoid the tidying up of the chaos of life into dishonest structures, "the lies of fiction" (*The Ice Is Singing*, p. 147). Anna, therefore, begins her personal diary and does so in the style that has already been established as that of Anna's voice. In other words, the writing here is transparent and in the documentary mode, and though the diary breaks off for the four years between 1950 and 1954 while Anna is undergoing psychoanalysis, it does so not because of a failure in the diary method but because the psychoanalyst, Mrs. Marks, has taken an interest in Anna's diary: "in making it part of her process, so to speak, she was robbing me of it" (p. 241). When Anna has worked through her period of psychoanalysis she resumes the diary as before.

The second movement in the Blue Notebook, and one that makes Anna reconsider her documentary method, is that precipitated by the ending of Anna's five-year relationship with Michael in September 1954: "he says I make up stories about our life together. I shall write down, as truthfully as I can every stage of a day. Tomorrow. When tomorrow ends I shall sit down and write" (p. 327). Although the resulting entry, that of 17 September 1954, is written in the same style as that of the previous entries, it is transposed to the present tense which, together with its great length, represents Anna's new self-consciousness about diary writing: "And now of course, I am wondering if the fact that I chose to be very conscious of everything that happened yesterday changed the shape of the day" (p. 327). Though the narrative may be a factual document, the concern here is for the shape of the narrative, the way in which a certain structure carries meaning. In the Yellow Notebook, Anna rejects her provisional plan for her autobiographical novel about Ella and Paul because of the teleological structure of the narrative, the way in which the structure of the work is governed by its ending: "the pattern of an affair, even one that has lasted five years and has been as close as a marriage, is seen in terms of what ends it. That is why all this is untrue" (p. 231). As an alternative structure, Anna proposes a diary-type record of "two full days, in every detail, one at the beginning of the affair, and one towards the end," but this is equally rejected because she "would still be instinctively isolating and emphasising the factors that destroyed the affair" (p. 231).

Anna does concede that it might be possible to record a diary without forcing a narrative form on it, the diary, in my terms, as an open and nonteleological structure which, in Lennox's terms, would challenge dominant structures of thought that see subjectivity as "male: single, unified, teleological" (Lennox, "Trends in Literary Theory," p. 67); but this too is rejected because, without an overall pattern, the diary entries would be "records of a simple unthinking happiness" which Anna equates with "chaos" (p. 231). Anna is, therefore, caught between the chaos or formlessness of daily events, that is, the factual truth of the diary and its emotional naivety, and a belief in writing as a visionary experience, the necessity for writing to provide a true overall perspective: "Literature is analysis after the event" (p. 231). Anna, therefore, rejects her own exhaustive account of a single day and resorts, like Marion in *The Ice Is Singing*, to the "list," or in Anna's case, the *journal externe*; for the next eighteen months the Blue Notebook is a strict record of daily events written in an abbreviated rather than a literary style and without reference to her thoughts and emotions: "Got up early. Read so-and-so. Saw so-and-so. Janet is sick. Janet is well. Molly is offered a part she likes/doesn't like, etc" (p. 455).

The third movement results from the abandonment of both the detailed record and the abbreviated record:

The Blue Notebook, which I had expected to be the most truthful of the notebooks, is worse than any of them. I expected a terse record of facts to present some sort of pattern when I read it over, but this sort of record is as false as the account of what happened on 15th September, 1954, which I read now embarrassed because of its emotionalism and because of its assumption that if I wrote "at nine-thirty I went to the lavatory to shit and at two to pee and at four I sweated," this would be more real than if I simply wrote what I thought. (p. 455)

The *journal externe* is equally empty of transcendent shape and truth, and the problem now for Anna is that her awareness of the formal properties of the diary, its failure to transcribe a meaningful reality, leaves her with a kind of existentialist nausea: "Every day I shaped Anna . . . and felt as if I had saved that day from chaos. Yet now I read those entries and feel nothing. I am increasingly affected by vertigo where words mean nothing. Words mean nothing" (p. 462). This is similar to the position in which Nelly Dean finds herself in *Nelly's Version*, when, after a brief exchange with a woman outside a shop, she notes: "I began to feel that I had lost touch, not only with places and events, but with human language also, since her last words had been flung down with all the assurance of a token that would be picked up and utilised. And yet I did not know what to do with it" (*Nelly's Version*, p. 34). Nelly decides that if she is to have any control at all over her life and exert some degree of "existential choice" ("most people have never experienced what it is like to function in a vacuum where one course of action might be just as meaningless or pregnant as any other" [p. 32]) then she has to fill this semantic void and make connections ("Everybody should have a story which is coherent, with a certain consistency" [p. 187]). For Anna, too, some sense of form is vital: "For words are form, and if I am at a pitch where shape, form, expression are nothing, then I am nothing, for it has become clear to me, reading the notebooks, that I remain Anna because of a certain kind of intelligence" (p. 463).

Yet given these similarities between the positions of Anna Wulf and Nelly Dean, there is one great difference. For Nelly Dean, her social identity is dependent upon the words she uses to describe herself, particularly gendered stereotypes such as wife and mother, and because such words are defined in relation to a privileged male term, while they give Nelly a sense of identity they also inevitably act to deny her an independent selfhood. Identity is gendered through language. For Anna Wulf, on the other hand, language does not control identity but rather acts as an index of the health of the intellect: "I remain Anna because of a certain kind of intelligence. This intelligence is dissolving and I am very frightened" (p. 463). In other words, the failure of the documentary strategy for Anna is not a failure of language but a failure of the integrity of the language user, the integrity of a humanist and antiexistentialist individualism that transcends language and cultural structures: "real experience can't be described. . . . The people who have been there, in the place in themselves where words, patterns, order, dissolve, will know what I mean and the others won't" (p. 609). Anna Wulf believes in an essential selfhood which transcends language. It is for this reason that Anna rejects preexisting forms and her psychoanalyst's attempts to have her account for her experiences in terms of mythic patterns:

. . . if I say to you: I recognise in that dream, such and such a myth; or in that emotion about my father, that folk-tale; or the atmosphere of that memory is the same as an English ballad—then you smile, you are satis-

fied. As far as you are concerned, I've gone beyond the childish, I've trans-
muted it and saved it, by embodying it in myth. (p. 456)

For the psychoanalyst, the satisfaction is in "The pleasure of recognition, of a bit of rescue-work, so to speak, rescuing the formless
into form. Another bit of chaos rescued and 'named'" (p. 457). Yet
for Anna this satisfaction is based on a terrible evasion: "during
these dreams, no matter what frightening material they incorporate, I could cry with happiness. And I know why—it's because all
the pain, and the killing and the violence is safely held in the story
and it can't hurt me" (p. 457). As Marion in *The Ice Is Singing* puts
it: "She names the pain. She identifies it, telling herself that thus it
can be remedied, later in the story" (p. 15). Once again we are back
to the comfort of storytelling, the false structure that belies the
transcendent experience.

The Blue Notebook, however, goes beyond the abandonment of
language that marks the end of *The Ice Is Singing* and becomes at
its end an account of painful experiences, particularly sexual experiences, that Anna must confront and from which she must free
herself rather than merely "name." The notebook then becomes an
account of her breakdown into "madness" ("These last three days I
have been inside madness" [p. 569]), the catalyst for which is her
violent relationship to the American, Saul Green, who comes to live
in her flat as a lodger. As Anna's *alter ego*, Ella, puts it: "A man and
a woman. . . . Both cracking up because of a deliberate attempt to
transcend their own limits. And out of the chaos, a new kind of
strength" (p. 454). The descent into madness, therefore, acts as a
prelude to the transcendence of the split into four different notebooks:

He said: "Why do you have four notebooks?" I said: "Obviously, because
it's been necessary to split myself up, but from now on I shall be using one
only." I was interested to hear myself say this, because until then I hadn't
known it. . . . There he stood, the American, clutching this history in both
hands for fear he would fall, hating me, the jailor. I said as I had said
before: "Don't you think it's extraordinary that we are both people whose
personalities, whatever that word may mean, are large enough to include
all sorts of things, politics and literature and art, but now that we're mad
everything concentrates down to one small thing, that I don't want you to
go off and sleep with someone else, and that you must lie to me about it?"
(pp. 576–77)

As Anna's personality implodes, so the Blue Notebook itself abandons both the dateline of the diary entries and the division between the entries: "I wrote the last sentence three days ago, but I didn't realise it was three days until I worked it out" (p. 542). This final strategy, the movement into the discursive mode, therefore represents a descent beyond time and place into madness ("We're inside a cocoon of madness" [p. 562]; "weeks of craziness and timelessness" [p. 609]), a madness that allows Anna somewhat paradoxically to go on writing, paradoxical because the experience remains beyond language: "there's nothing there, just words on paper, I can't communicate, even to myself when I read it back, the knowledge of destruction as a force" (p. 568). This experience of "the real movement of the world towards dark, hardening power" (p. 568) marks the lowest point in Anna's madness, a point that Martens describes as the experience of "pure presence" (*The Diary Novel*, p. 244) and which, if Martens is correct, finally contrasts *The Golden Notebook* with existentialist fiction. And as Anna moves toward recovery, she abandons even the intercalated or periodic structure of the diary, so that the final notebook, the Golden Notebook, becomes not a diary at all but a retrospective testament to the new strength of vision that has allowed Anna to regain control of her identity.

In the context of a discussion of liberation through diary writing, it remains necessary to comment on the way in which Anna achieves her breakthrough. Two connected aspects are of particular importance: the way in which Anna finds her integrated vision through dreams and the discourse of fantasy; and the way that this resolution is achieved through a sexual relationship:

I slept and I dreamed the dream. This time there was no disguise anywhere. I was the malicious male-female dwarf figure, the principle of joy-in-destruction; and Saul was my counter-part, male-female, my brother and my sister, and we were dancing in some open space, under enormous white buildings, which were filled with hideous, menacing, black machinery which held destruction. But in the dream, he and I, or she and I, were friendly, we were not hostile, we were together in spiteful malice. There was a terrible yearning nostalgia in the dream, the longing for death. (pp. 573–74)

This "yearning nostalgia" for destruction and death is what had made Anna dissatisfied with *Frontiers of War*, her novel about her wartime experiences in Central Africa: "a lying nostalgia, a longing for licence, for freedom, for the jungle, for formlessness" (p. 82). Here, however, Anna is embracing formlessness and working through her terror of destruction ("the real nerve-terror of the nightmare" [p. 568]), rather than evading it by "naming." One of the complexities of *The Golden Notebook* is the way in which certain negative concepts are not abandoned but recur with a positive implication. The concept of breakdown, as has been pointed out by Martens, is used both positively and negatively: "'formlessness' becomes the solution to false order and therefore the opposite of chaos" (*The Diary Novel*, p. 240). This is true also of the intellect, which struggles to prevent Anna's healing breakdown and yet when the breakdown comes guides Anna through it ("the part of my mind which, I knew, was the disinterested personality who had saved me from disintegration" [593]). And it is true of the notion of storytelling or "naming," which until this point in the book has been equated with evasion:

I had to "name" the frightening things over and over, in a terrible litany; like a sort of disinfection by the conscious mind before I slept. But now, asleep, it was not making past events harmless, by naming them, *but making sure they were still there.* Yet I know that having made sure they were still there, I would have to "name" them in a different way, and that was why the controlling personality was forcing me back. (p. 594)

In her mind, therefore, Anna must move beyond her previous reworkings of her past: "I was faced with the burden of recreating order out of the chaos that my life had become. Time had gone, and my memory did not exist, . . . and I knew that what I had invented was all false" (p. 597). Fantasy and the discursive mode therefore become for Anna a way of freeing herself, if only in a limited way, from the terror of dissolution and destruction by confronting and acknowledging it; and such a strategy is similar to that of the female diarists of *The Bad Sister* and *Three*, particularly the way in which the process of liberation involves transcending the male–female division: "Saul was my counter-part, male-female, my brother and my sister" (p. 573). Yet, although there are such similarities, there are important differences in the use of fantasy in *The Golden Notebook*.

First, the Blue Notebook is written in such a way that there is no uncertainty between fantasy and reality—Anna's dreams are all recounted retrospectively from a point of relative sanity outside the dreams. The notebook is selective ("of the happiness, the normality, the laughter, not a word will be written" [p. 566]) as well as intercalated or periodic, yet the factuality of what it reports is unquestioned. Anna does not become for herself "the malicious male-female dwarf figure" (p. 573), the variation on Mr. Hyde that Jane Wild becomes in *The Bad Sister*, and fantasy does not represent an autonomous mode of discourse as it does in both Quin and Tennant: it remains controlled by the documentary mode. Nor does it represent a new and avant-garde form that the novel must take if it is to avoid the untruths of conventional fiction: as Martens points out, Lessing never doubts "that it is the purpose of language to be referential" (*The Diary Novel,* p. 244). Rather, fantasy, like the diary styles, remains part of the overall variation of styles in *The Golden Notebook.* This variation of styles traces the process of finding a new unified form, a process caused primarily by Anna's own sense of fragmentation. As Anna reflects at the opening of the notebooks: "I am incapable of writing the only kind of novel which interests me: a book powered with an intellectual or moral passion strong enough to create order, to create a new way of looking at life. It is because I am too diffused" (p. 80). Both fantasy and the diary form participate in Anna's attempt to create a visionary order, an order that, with the writing of the fifth notebook, the Golden Notebook, results in the control of fantasy and the abandonment of the diary format.

Second, the movement into wholeness is marked by a fantasy of a sexual relationship which somehow transcends sexual division ("Saul was my counter-part, male-female, my brother and my sister"), as in Tennant and Quin, yet this movement beyond sexual difference is representative rather than the essence of what Anna Wulf must face up to in order to attain liberation. *The Golden Notebook* is certainly about the place of women in society, the women who are driven to drink because of their treatment by their husbands, the women who are castigated by society because they remain unmarried; yet the novel views the emotional relationship between the sexes as an index of a more general malaise in society: "In a world as terrible as this, limit emotion" (p. 528). As Barbara Bellow Watson puts it: "the woman's point of view is nonetheless a paradigm of the fragmentation in contemporary life and a paradigm also of the failure of sets and systems to respond helpfully to human questions" ("Leaving the Safety of Myth," p. 13). Thus, in the way that the Blue Notebook deals with the failure of sexual relationships, the Black Notebook deals with a cultural sterility and the Red Notebook with political sterility. Saul Green is not, therefore, merely representative of men but is also a writer and a political activist. While it is true that he has acted as a catalyst in Anna's breakthrough through breakdown ("a sort of inner conscience or critic" [p. 598]), Anna's overcoming of her sexual jealousy ("All that was finished" [p. 608]; "I felt towards him as if he were my brother" [p. 617]) results also both in an artistic breakthrough, Anna writing her novella "Free Women," and in a political breakthrough, her final rejection of "the communist conformity" and acceptance of a heroic political individualism: "Very few people really care about freedom, about liberty, about the truth, very few. Very few people have guts, the kind of guts on which a real democracy has to depend" (p. 548).

Lastly, the kind of liberation Anna achieves, though it shares some of the mysticism of the liberation achieved by the female diarists in *The Bad Sister* and *Three*, does not result as in those cases in death even though Anna may at moments long for death. Instead, the movement of the novel is towards an ironical freedom, a freedom that makes it possible for Anna to live with the constraints on her freedom and accept the presence of dissolution in the world: "once having been there, there's a terrible irony, a terrible shrug of the shoulders, and it's not a question of fighting it, or disowning it, or of right or wrong, but simply knowing it is there, always" (pp. 609–10). Like Sisyphus's, Anna's task is impossible, yet she must continue to try to push a boulder up the mountain of human stupidity knowing that it will only roll back down again: "I'm not for sainthood, I'm going to be a boulder-pusher" (p. 604). Freedom for Anna may be the result of a new strength of vision but that vision remains that of someone concerned passionately with life on earth.

The five women diarists I have dealt with in this chapter all suffer psychological breakdowns: two of them (Rogers and Figes) keep diaries in the aftermath of their breakdowns, two (Tennant and Quin) deal with the movement towards breakdown, and one (Lessing) deals with the build up to breakdown and the passage through breakdown. Writing of *The Golden Notebook* in the article from which I have already quoted, Watson argues that "Women in our time have become experts in fragmentation. Fragmentation is the essential theme of women's consciousness" ("Leaving the Safety of Myth," p. 23). Thus, to adapt the remark by Tennant's Jane Wild when she looks at herself in the mirror ("Women and mirrors; mirrors and women"): Women and breakdowns; breakdowns and women.

This leads on to the relationship between diaries and breakdown. Each of the works discussed above deals with a need to escape a domestic incarceration seen in terms of a stereotyped male–female relationship, a cultural opposition that, as K. K. Ruthven points out, is analogous to other binary oppositions such as right–left or good–evil, all of which privilege the first term (*Feminist Literary Studies*, p. 14). The failure of this opposition to offer women a workable identity results both in the woman's psychological breakdown and the drive for freedom. The diary then becomes a means by which the woman tries to make sense of her shifting perception of reality, either in the documentary mode or in the discursive mode.

However, we need now to assess the relative merits of these modes for women novelists. I have already questioned at the beginning of this chapter the degree to which the diary strategy itself is necessarily questioning Lennox's "dominant structures of thought," or is necessarily as Martens suggests a subversion of a dominant (male) narrative structure and a reflection of the fragmented, open, and nonteleological structure of women's lives. *The Ice Is Singing* concerns itself with the latter ("My life goes on, shapelessly, raggedly, from day to day" [p. 153]) yet still presents a self-contained fiction and a supporting narrative argument, and is both a closed and a teleological structure. Once more quoting Lennox: "feminist content without a new feminist form is of little use, for conventional forms merely preserve the epistemological categories of male discourse" ("Trends in Literary Theory," p. 64). The fictive diary has a long tradition to it and may, like any fiction, be either conventional or subversive of the literary norms of its times; it is not of itself one of those "radical and disruptive literary forms" (p. 67) for which Lennox calls.

It seems a little invidious to pick out *The Ice Is Singing* to demonstrate what must be a real difficulty facing women who write fictive women's diaries today, namely, that the association between women, diaries, and psychological breakdown almost dictates the content of the novel. Yet it has to be admitted that *The Ice Is Singing* does not mark a development in diary fiction or in the relationship between men and women. The diarist trying to come to terms with a loss of identity caused by the desertion of her husband and the new-found independence of her teenage children is a reworking of the situation of the diarist's namesake, Marion, a minor character in *The Golden Notebook*. This is not to say that *The Ice Is Singing* has no cultural value (and the echo in its title of another novel by Lessing, *The Grass Is Singing*, acknowledges the homage it pays to Lessing); neither does this reworking mean that it has no relevance to the lives of many women today. Yet its conclusion that the diary must be abandoned because it falsifies reality is somewhat simplistic given that it is also arguing that the diary form itself accurately documents the fragmentation of breakdown and the formlessness of women's lives.

The confusion seems to lie in a belief that the open form of the nonfiction diary (which of course in practice differs itself in its degree of openness) automatically results in a diary novel with an open form. Thus, Watson talks of the four main notebooks of *The Golden Notebook* as "an open system, not a closed one": "The Notebooks are inductive, open. Reality, extremely unmanageable, arrives and is admitted. There will be no conclusions until the data are all in" ("Leaving the Safety of Myth," p. 32). Yet it is not the notebooks themselves that question the form of the novel in *The Golden Notebook*, but the status of the novella "Free Women" which, while it serves to give a narrative coherence to *The Golden Notebook* as a whole, is written in an ironic tone by one of the characters within the work. The notebooks themselves are fully comprehensible as notebooks kept by Anna Wulf, and the diary form of *The Golden Notebook* questions reality only from inside the conventions of realism. The point about Quin, Tennant, and Figes, then, is that in contrast to Rogers and Lessing these writers not only challenge the stereotyped position of women in Western culture but do so by also challenging the dominant literary mode of the diary novel, that of a closed and teleological documentary realism. In other words, the reality of gender differences is seen as having a demonstrable interactive relationship with the writing of reality.

In the case of Quin's *Three*, the movement away from realism is contained in an experimentation with the language of the novel, the three different narrative styles moving progressively away from a documentary referentiality. The function of this stylistic experimentation is to represent the way the diarist S progressively frees herself from the stifling domesticity of Ruth and Leonard, a couple locked into mutually antagonistic male–female roles. S is finally held to have attained a mode of being that, in transcending reality, transcends sexual difference. Much the same can be said for Tennant's *The Bad Sister*, where the transcendence of sexual difference is likewise represented by a discourse that is antirealistic, realism in this case being equated with the editorial matter that frames yet cannot give a unified meaning to Jane Wild's diary. And in questioning sexual identity, both works also question the integrity of the realist character and the assumption that one character is essentially different from another.

The structure of *Nelly's Version* is also open and antirealist in the illogicality of Nelly's coming to read in a public library not only the novel in which she is a character, but also different versions of the novel. In other words, though Nelly may continue to write in the documentary mode, the novel adopts the discursive mode. As I pointed out in my discussion of *Nelly's Version* above, this internal frame-breaking demonstrates the argument of the novel that identity is dependent upon gendered stereotypes which are prescribed by the texts of society, and that in a male-dominated society the models of selfhood offered to women will be subservient to those of men. Yet in making the point, *Nelly's Version* goes further and also uses the technique adopted in Tennant, that of merging characters, Nelly becoming at the end the old woman she meets at the beginning of the novel. To be sure, both Lessing and Rogers question the boundaries between the diarist and fictional projections of the diarist, yet this remains an argument within a text which depends on a documentary realism and a representational division between art and life: both Anna Wulf and Marion remain formally differentiated from either Ella or any of Marion's fictive characters. In all five novels dealt with in this chapter it may be argued that it is realism as a mode of writing that is seen as limiting the freedom of women, that is, the way in which realism cannot reflect the totality of reality; yet only in Figes, Quin, and Tennant does the examination of individual identity lead to a radical attempt to write an alternative discourse, to interrogate, as Mary Jacobus puts it, "the limits of meaning."

Which leaves us with a surplus, the association of women with diaries and where to locate the specifically feminist strategy within the text. It is tempting to conclude that those diary novels written by women that deal with women's issues combine an ungendered narrative form with a feminist content. We could, therefore, argue that the difference between, say, Figes's *Nelly's Version* and Malcolm Lowry's "Through the Panama," dealt with in the previous chapter, is one of content rather than form; and it is also possible in practice to read Quin, Figes, and Tennant in terms of a movement toward experimentalism and antirealism within the British novel as whole, placing Quin and Figes alongside B. S. Johnson, Alan Burns, and Giles Gordon, with Tennant a little later alongside Ian McEwan, Martin Amis, and Angela Carter. Nevertheless, what I have tried to demonstrate is that, while realism is not essentially masculine and antirealism essentially feminine, different styles, forms, and modes of writing can be aligned with gender differences through the use of contrast. Thus, the antirealism of Jane Wild's diary in *The Bad Sister* is associated with a feminist discourse through contrast with the rationalist realism of the editorial frame, and, though the editor is never identified as male, it is not possible in context to read the editor as a woman. Similarly, *Nelly's Version* dramatizes a conflict between a culturally dominant masculine realism and an alternative mode of writing that is necessary if women are to be freed from merely playing out stereotyped roles. While some degree of documentary realism is necessary in all these works as a touchstone for making the alignment between gender and discourse, the novels by Figes, Quin, and Tennant show us how developments in the written form of the diary novel can now be used to demonstrate not only a breakdown in the received perception of reality but also the unstable dependence of that reality on a particular mode of writing. Women, diaries, and breakdown all come together in writing the difference.

Writing and Reality: Conclusion

The relationship between writing and reality—or, more specifically, between the novel and reality—is one that has been viewed in a number of different and contradictory ways. This relationship is seen variously as one in which reality exceeds literary realism, always outstripping the representation of reality in fiction ("The actuality is continually outdoing our talents"); as one in which realism is itself necessarily more real than antirealism, since it remains the dominant mode of representation ("most of us continue to live most of our lives on the assumption that the reality which realism imitates actually exists"); as one in which the notion of reality is itself a fictional construct, a way of imposing order on chaos ("even to seek an explanation represents a denial of chaos"); and one in which changes in the literary representation of reality will allow extratextual reality to be redefined ("new forms will reveal new things in reality").[1] It is symptomatic of this confusion that Ian Watt in *The Rise of the Novel* is able to argue two mutually exclusive points of view. On the one hand, "formal realism" in the novel is "only a convention" and "there is no reason why the report on human life which is presented by it should be in fact any truer than those presented through the very different conventions of other literary genres" (p. 35). On the other hand, Watt argues that the "largely referential use of language" to be found in formal realism "allows a more immediate imitation of individual experience"

(p. 35), a "close and detailed correspondence to real life" (p. 36). In other words, Watt is ambivalent about whether formal realism corresponds to an extratextual reality or whether it is primarily a literary convention that only appears to. The problem here is in the concept of imitation, for, even if imitation proceeds only through conventions, imitation also presupposes an imitation of something else, and what is that something else but "life itself?"

In applying Watt's notion of formal realism to the diary novel, H. Porter Abbott splits the conventions that support the illusion of the real into two types: "The artless spontaneity of the internal, non-retrospective record is one. The other is the document itself, which, as a *document*, claims to be real" (*Diary Fiction*, p. 19). This division is not so discrete as Abbott suggests, since a correlative of artless spontaneity may be an abbreviated linguistic style, itself a feature of the diary as document. Nevertheless, there is a sense in which the fictive document is an imitation of reality different in kind from an internalized record and, as Abbott himself points out, efforts to go beyond the diary strategy in portraying internalized reality have only been achieved "by employing narrative devices— monologue, interior monologue—that are necessarily fictive" (p. 19). The diary as document is therefore "a kind of realistic absolute or terminal point" (p. 19), a point beyond which the representation of thought becomes more obviously artful. We enter here the realm of Lorna Martens' quasi-diary.

What I want to suggest now is that, whatever the problems of imitation in Watt's notion of formal realism, we have in Abbott's application of formal realism a clearly defined imitation: the diary novel imitates the form of the nonfiction diary. Moreover, though the fictive document is dependent on literary conventions, its imitation is in the form of direct mimicry: it is an imitation of a nonfiction discourse rather than an imitation of a different order of signification, the world "outside" written discourse. As Patricia Waugh puts it, "Metafictional texts show that literary fiction can never imitate or 'represent' the world but always imitates or 'represents' the discourses which in turn construct that world" (*Metafiction*, p. 100). This is not, however, to reconstitute the division between inside and outside, realism and reality, that is the source of Watt's confusion and which to some extent undercuts Waugh's larger project: as I have argued throughout this book there is no absolute division, and difference itself relies on the relationship between opposing terms. What I have been arguing is that a culture categorizes and privileges certain types of discourse, such as occurs in the division between nonfiction and fiction, and that literary forms participate directly in the structuring of a society. In *Nineteen Eighty-Four*, the relationship between Winston Smith and the state is, therefore, paralleled by the relationship between his diary and the official discourse of the state. The broader point is not so much who writes reality but the way in which different types of discourse are categorized and validated.

It is clear, therefore, that in challenging the difference between certain categories of discourse, modern British diary fiction has over the past thirty or so years been challenging in varying degrees the boundaries by which reality has been culturally validated. Thus we have seen in the previous chapters works that examine the relationship between fact and fiction, the relationship between private and public and the status of history, the relationship between writer and reader and the limits of a knowable autobiographical selfhood, and the relationship between masculine and feminine discourse. And despite some explicit statements by the writers themselves, the effective basis of this challenge has not been the division between literature and an extratextual reality that is there to be imitated but the interdependence of writing and reality, the way in which social reality depends on the relationship between discourses. As Waugh puts it, "Metafictional deconstruction has . . . offered extremely accurate models for understanding the contemporary experience of the world as a construction, as an artifice, a web of interdependent semiotic systems" (p. 9). It is the imitation of the diary as a private, factual, and written document that becomes the key element in this challenge to an unmediated reality.

What remains to be done here is to offer an overview of those works previously discussed according to the degree to which they use the imitation of a diary to challenge the boundaries between discourses and, by implication, to challenge the values attached to the diary when viewed as a transcription of reality.

Robin Maugham's *The Last Encounter* offers little challenge to social reality. The view it presents of history is an imperialist one, one in which the heroic individual struts the stage and is the prime mover in international affairs. As Paul Carter puts it, "Imperial history's mythic lineage of heroes is the consequence of its theatrical assumption that, in reality, historical individuals are actors, fulfilling a higher destiny" (*The Road to Botany Bay*, p. xvii). Maugham's diary novel cultivates rather than challenges the personality cult of contemporary political activity and does so by attempting to efface the difference between fact and fiction through a series of documents that attest to the authenticity of General Gordon's diary. Similar attestation is incorporated into John Berger's *A Painter of Our Time*, an editor named John acting to interpret for the reader the role of the artist in the making of contemporary history. Berger's Marxist model of history is very different from Maugham's imperial history, but it is nevertheless similarly based both on a strongly referential notion of writing and on the assumed factuality of the account. As a referential document, the diary is a piece of historical evidence. The same reliance on referentiality is true of John Fowles's *The Collector*, where the diary is once more carefully framed and attested as nonfiction. Like the imprisoned Miranda Grey, it too is collected and subordinated. Moreover, in all three cases, a nonfiction model reinforces the formal realism of the diary and its status as a real document: in Maugham, reference is made to the published diaries of General Gordon; in Berger, the model is the diary Gauguin kept in Tahiti (p. 145); and in Fowles, Miranda Grey refers specifically to the diary of Anne Frank (p. 233).

The formal realism of the diary and other documents is employed in Robert Nye's *The Voyage of the Destiny*, a work that, if it reinforces imperial history and the notion of a higher destiny, also disrupts authenticity by anachronism. In other words, its formal realism is that of a modern diary rather than a sixteenth-century diary, a feature that contrasts with the public documents included within it. Such a strategy is problematical for while the novel may be challenging the accuracy of received history, it does so by a method that both effaces an authentic sixteenth-century style and draws attention to its own fictivity. The challenge is therefore tempered by an insistence on the greater truth of fiction. A similar problem occurs with William Golding's *Rites of Passage*: while the language and surface form may be authentic, the underlying form is that of the late eighteenth-century letter-journal novel. Golding's trilogy, as I pointed out in Chapter 7, does locate changes in literary practice against changes in social structure, but the fictive model largely reenacts this change without disturbing contemporary structures.

Both Nye and Golding, and to some extent Fowles, question the competence of writing to interpret reality, but they do so thematically rather than structurally. We find the diarists reassessing their previous interpretation of events without assessing the language of their diaries as a medium for self-assessment. As Gavin Edwards has pointed out, quoting an unpublished essay by Martin

Golding, this process of self-assessment is essentially moralistic, viewing life as a kind of narrative along which the individual travels, periodically testing and reviewing his or her behaviour ("Narrative," p. 116). Such a thematization of the relationship between writing and reality is central to Margaret Forster's *Private Papers* and Iris Murdoch's *The Sea, The Sea* in both of which the diarist/autobiographer is forced to take moral stock of her or his life when brought to face an alternative discourse and an alternative interpretation. The formal realism here, though, operates to set limits to this challenge, the contradictions themselves making the diaries more rather than less authentic as documents. In Abbott's words, "As readers, we no longer ask our diarist to give a wholly sincere account of her feelings" (*Diary Fiction*, p. 21). The challenge is to the truthfulness or sincerity of the diarist rather than to the diary as a referential document. The diary remains an unproblematic record of insincerity.

This thematization of the problem of recording reality is taken to the limits of referentiality by Doris Lessing in *The Golden Notebook* and by her protégée, Jane Rogers, in *The Ice Is Singing*. In both works the diary is placed alongside fiction that reworks some of the characters and events recorded in the diary, the implication being that reality exceeds the realist devices of the diary to record it. True reality can only be suggested by conflicting types of discourse, the diary tending toward fiction, the novel and short story leaving fictivity for truth. Nevertheless, in both works fact and fiction remain largely discrete with the diary framing the fiction, and only at the end of *The Golden Notebook* is there a structural conflict, when it is suggested that the framing authorial narrative may be part of a novel written by the diarist. Throughout Rogers, therefore, and throughout most of Lessing, the diary provides what is seen as the raw material of the fiction, and though the conclusion in both cases is that the diary is an inaccurate imitation of reality because of a failure in language itself, there is no breakdown of the boundaries of discourse within the structure of the novels. Reality remains somehow beyond language, in the silence beyond the diary.

Patricia Waugh has suggested that contemporary metafiction has questioned the adequacy of realism in two separate ways:

What has to be acknowledged is that there are two poles of metafiction: one that finally accepts a substantial real world whose significance is not entirely composed of relationships within language; and one that suggests there can never be an escape from the prisonhouse of language and either delights or despairs in this. (*Metafiction*, p. 53)

In the first category, Waugh places Fowles, Lessing, and Vonnegut, and this suggests that the first half of my review of modern British diary fiction corresponds to Waugh's first pole of metafiction. Certainly, what I have been arguing is that those works I have so far reviewed do focus on a diarist acting and reacting in a "substantial real world." In other words, the use of formal realism is primarily to efface the work's textuality. This does not mean that there is no questioning of the relationship between writing and reality, and Lessing is very far from Maugham. However, the challenge is thematic, it is enacted through the diary as a mode of self-assessment; as readers, we are asked to believe in the diary as an authentic document. It is, perhaps, not surprising to find in this category most of those works that question the objectivity of historical discourse since history is dealt with as a question of interpretation rather than ontology.

Waugh's second pole, Frederic Jameson's prisonhouse of language, also seems relevant to certain of those works which, I would argue, disrupt the formal realism of the diary novel. Ann Quin's *Three* and Emma Tennant's *The Bad Sister* both depart from the formal realism of the diary to present a fantasy discourse that sharply undercuts the referentiality of the diary. In both cases fantasy is presented as a specifically feminine discourse which counters the rationality and logic of a masculine realism: in Quin, one of the diaries is taperecorded, while in Tennant the diary borders on the interior monologue or quasi-diary found extensively in B. S. Johnson's *Trawl*. Moreover, in all three cases there is extended language play and a use of word association that is antireferential or even superreferential, a feature Waugh herself associates with her second category where writers "conduct their fictional experiments even at the level of the *sign*" (p. 53). These writers would seem to have gone beyond Abbott's "realistic absolute or terminal point" in their employment of fictional techniques. The diary is less recognizably a diary.

However, the prisonhouse of language idea is of questionable widespread use for my purposes both because it relies on the questionable inside/outside dichotomy and because it focusses on language rather than on types of discourse. The alternative polarity I would propose is between those novels that examine the relationship between writing and reality thematically through a formal imitation of the diary, and those that examine that relationship through structural contradiction. These are, of course, poles rather than discrete categories and both Eva Figes' *Nelly's Version* and Rayner Heppenstall's *The Pier*, for example, clearly mimic the diary form; yet what brings them closer to Quin and Tennant and contrasts them with Golding is the way in which the form and its referentiality is contradicted internally by the novel's structure. In Figes, the central character produces from a library shelf versions of the novel in which she herself appears; in Heppenstall, the narrator similarly traces in his diaries the emergence of a plot for a novel which is actually *The Pier*.

What we can identify here is the collapse of the divisions between discourses upon which those works discussed in the earlier half of this review depended. Russell Hoban's *Turtle Diary* and Ann Quin's *Passages* offer joint narratives that like Margaret Forster's question thematically at the level of the narrator's thoughts the possibility of recording reality in a diary. The ironical effect, however, of events forcing the diarist to reassess his or her previous interpretation is paralleled in Hoban and Quin—but not in Forster—by a structural irony, an irony that undercuts the use of the diary in fiction itself. Linguistic parallels destabilize the narratives and suggest not so much a boundary between fiction and nonfiction as an unstable relativity. The adequacy of the diary as a vehicle for self-assessment is displaced first from the sincerity of the narrator to Abbott's notion of the authenticity of the narrative; but this authenticity is more radically displaced by a further irony—both fiction and nonfiction are shown to be dependent on a textuality that exceeds the difference between fiction and fact. This contradiction still depends on a recognition of the diary strategy, on the possibility of formal realism, but it can no longer be contained at that level. These diaries cannot be read as authentic documents.

In this sense, we can propose that at the pole most distant from Maugham is Malcolm Lowry's "Through the Panama." Here, all the elements of the diary mimicked by diary fiction are systematically contradicted by the structure of the work: the possibility that the work is nonretrospective is exceeded by annotation and a divergence into twin narratives; the first-person record is undercut by a shifting of the diarist's identity; and the intercalated nature of the record is disrupted by alternative entries for the same day. The result is a work that is comprised of a number of discourses none of which can contain any of the others, and the stability that the formal realism of diary fiction promises is systematically questioned.

Thus Lowry, Quin, Tennant, B. S. Johnson, Figes, Heppenstall, and Hoban are not only questioning at the thematic level but ultimately demonstrating at the level of structure the instability of those generic boundaries by which a culture legitimates and privileges certain forms of discourse.

Two questions have still to be faced. The first is the question of why major British writers have chosen to examine the relationship between writing and reality, be it thematically or structurally, through diary fiction. The second question is how far this challenge has been effective.

It is arguable, I believe, that the period in which these novelists were working has been a period in which there has been no consensus notion of reality, and reality has therefore been contestable. Hence the many and often self-contradictory statements by these and other writers about the relationship between the novel and reality, statements, it needs be added, that display more a polemical than a literary purpose and which can hardly ever be demonstrated in the novels themselves. Nevertheless, the widespread choice of the diary form can be explained by its apparent closeness to reality. Given Lorna Martens' argument that the diary strategy is now no longer necessary or even adequate to represent thought processes, the function of the diary form is to signify a nonfiction discourse that has a higher reality-value than the fiction in which it appears. This is not necessarily the anachronism Martens suggests: "Considering that separate categories for fiction and nonfiction are being questioned particularly today . . . a legitimation for fiction that gives it the trappings of 'fact' would be more than superfluous" (*The Diary Novel*, p. 189). It is surely the possibility that the novel itself can be read as nonfiction that makes an undermining of the difference between fiction and nonfiction effective. What the diary form here engages with is, as Martens points out earlier, the modern suspicion that the novel imposes a false order on reality (p. 186). Moreover, the diary as an effective record of reality is closely associated with such liberal values as individuality, sincerity, common sense, and the importance of "the little incidents of daily life"; the diary, in this case, provides a field in which to reassert or challenge those values depending on the degree to which the diary strategy is effective as a mode of self-assessment. In a period in which the liberal humanist view of reality has been threatened by such contrasting ideologies as Marxism, existentialism, and structuralism (taking structuralism as an ideology that

undermines humanism from within, as in Lacanian psychoanalysis), the diary, which has long been read according to the assumptions of liberal humanism, has to be confronted. It is no longer
quite enough to laugh politely at that irritating Victorian nobody,
Mr Pooter, or that spotty adolescent, Adrian Mole.

The question of Adrian Mole leads us into the second question
of how far this challenge has been effective in renegotiating the
boundaries of discourse by which reality is culturally validated.
Sue Townsend's Adrian Mole books, acclaimed for their "accuracy,"
continue to be best-sellers. Two aspects of this issue present themselves. The first is that, as I mentioned in my introduction, the
radical reworking of diary fiction seems to have come to an end,
being a product largely of changes in society from the mid-1950s to
the mid-1970s. This suggests that such formalized literary experiments are no longer felt to be culturally relevant. The undermining
of a commonsense extratextual reality now seems to be considered
of little use either to those confronting social issues such as the role
of women in society, as in Rogers and Forster, or in the discourse of
a resurgent and popular liberalism, as in Townsend.

The second aspect is that the internal strategy of these novels do
not so much suggest a new type of discourse as themselves rely on
the formal realism of the diary mode. Contradiction relies on two
positions being held simultaneously, and it is therefore possible to
see them, as Patricia Waugh does, as texts that deconstruct semiotic systems. Thus, the criticism of deconstruction might be held to
apply to the experimental diary novel, namely its failure to replace
the procedure it destabilizes. Christopher Norris, quoting Richard
Rorty, has pointed out how deconstruction can be aligned with one
of two divergent traditions in philosophy, one being a pursuit of
truth through rationality, the other being a radical skepticism of
the basis of this philosophical enquiry, namely writing. The conclusion is that the differing aims of these two traditions leaves them
unable to replace each other. It is wrong to see them as alternatives, and, according to Norris, skeptical philosophers like Derrida
"have never pretended that life could be conducted in a practical
way if everyone acted consistently on sceptical assumptions"
(*Deconstruction*, p. 128). We might argue similarly that novelists
like Figes, Quin, and Lowry are not in the end seriously advocating
a universal shift to the post-structuralist diary.

It may finally be that to view modern British diary fiction as an
attempt to radically renegotiate reality, as I have been suggesting,
is to make too large a claim for it. Certainly it has been skeptical of

writing as a mode of transcribing reality, but if we see these works as a way of challenging the dominance of a rationalist realism without seeking to replace it we can claim that, though such writing may in one sense be marginal, in another sense it is central. For what all these works do, either thematically or structurally, is to reaffirm, first, the basis of fiction as a linguistic construct and, second, the way in which fiction demonstrates the conventionality of all written representations of reality. By choosing to reflect skeptically on the diary, modern British diary fiction has sought to remind us of the broader dimensions of the relationship between writing and reality. In so doing it graphically outlines the dangers both for the individual and for society as a whole that attend our setting too narrow a limit on that relationship.

NOTE

1. Philip Roth, "Writing American Fiction," p. 34; David Lodge, "The Novelist at the Crossroads," p. 109; B. S. Johnson, "Introduction to *Aren't You Rather Young to be Writing Your Memoirs?*," p. 156; Michel Butor, "The Novel as Research," p. 50; all in Malcolm Bradbury, *The Novel Today.*

Bibliography

Unless otherwise indicated, the place of publication is London.

PRIMARY SOURCES

I. Diary Fiction

Bellow, Saul. *Dangling Man*. 1944. Harmondsworth: Penguin, 1963.

Berger, John. *A Painter of Our Time*. 1958. Writers and Readers, 1976.

Butor, Michel. *Passing Time*. 1957. Faber, 1961.

Chapman, Robin. *The Duchess's Diary*. Faber, 1985.

Figes, Eva. *Nelly's Version*. 1977. Hamish Hamilton, 1985. Fontana, 1988.

Forster, Margaret. *Private Papers*. 1986. Harmondsworth: Penguin, 1987.

Fowles, John. *The Collector*. 1963. Pan, 1965.

Golding, William. *Rites of Passage*. 1980. Faber, 1982.

———. *Close Quarters*. 1987. Faber, 1988.

———. *Fire Down Below*. Faber, 1989.

———. *To the Ends of the Earth: A Sea Trilogy*. Faber, 1991. [Contains all three novels above.]

Heppenstall, Rayner. *The Pier*. Allison & Busby, 1986.

Hoban, Russell. *Turtle Diary*. 1975. Picador, 1977.

Johnson, B. S. *Travelling People*. Constable, 1963.

———. *Trawl*. 1966. Panther, 1968.

Lessing, Doris. *The Golden Notebook*. 1962. Frogmore, Herts: Panther, 1973.

————. *The Diaries of Jane Somers*. 1984. Harmondsworth: Penguin, 1985.

Lowry, Malcolm. "Through the Panama." In *Hear Us O Lord From Heaven Thy Dwelling Place*. 1961. Harmondsworth: Penguin, 1979. 26-98.

Lurie, Alison. *Real People*. 1969. Heinemann, 1970.

Maugham, Robin. *The Last Encounter*. Allen, 1972.

Murdoch, Iris. *The Sea, The Sea*. 1978. Triad Grafton, 1980.

Nye, Robert. *The Voyage of the Destiny*. 1982. Harmondsworth: Penguin, 1983.

Quin, Ann. *Three*. Calder & Boyars, 1966.

————. *Passages*. Calder & Boyars, 1969.

Rogers, Jane. *The Ice Is Singing*. Faber, 1987.

Sartre, Jean-Paul. *Nausea*. 1938. Harmondsworth: Penguin, 1965.

Somers, Jane [Doris Lessing]. *The Diary of a Good Neighbour*. Michael Joseph, 1983.

Tennant. Emma. *The Bad Sister*. 1978. Picador, 1979.

Townsend, Sue. *The Secret Diary of Adrian Mole*. Methuen, 1982.

Updike, John. *A Month of Sundays*. New York: Knopf, 1975.

Vonnegut, Kurt. *Mother Night*. 1961. Vintage, 1992.

II. Nonfiction Diaries

Bagnold, Enid. *A Diary Without Dates*. 1918. Virago, 1978.

Calder, Angus, and Dorothy Sheridan, eds. *Speak for Yourself: A Mass-Observation Anthology 1937–1949*. 1984. Oxford: Oxford UP, 1985.

Cullwick, Hannah. *The Diaries of Hannah Cullwick: Victorian Maidservant*. Ed. Liz Stanley. Virago, 1984.

Gordon, Charles George. *General Gordon's Khartoum Journal*. Ed. Lord Elton. Kimber, 1961.

Greene, Graham. *In Search of a Character: Two African Journals*. 1961. Harmondsworth: Penguin, 1968.

Heppenstall, Rayner. *The Master Eccentric: The Journals of Rayner Heppenstall 1969–81*. Ed. Jonathan Goodman. Allison & Busby, 1986.

Orton, Joe. *The Orton Diaries*. Ed. John Lahr. Methuen, 1986.

Waugh, Evelyn. *The Diaries of Evelyn Waugh*. Ed. Michael Davie. 1976. Harmondsworth: Penguin, 1979.

Woolf, Virginia. *A Writer's Diary*. Ed. Leonard Woolf. 1953. Frogmore, Herts: Triad/Panther, 1978.

III. Other Primary Sources

Berger, John. *Permanent Red*. 1960. Methuen, 1969.

Bradbury, Malcolm. *The History Man*. 1975. Arrow, 1977.

Fowles, John. *The French Lieutenant's Women*. Cape, 1969.

Greene, Graham. *A Burnt-Out Case.* 1960: Penguin, 1963.

Hogg, James. *The Private Memoirs and Confessions of a Justified Sinner.* 1824. Harmondsworth: Penguin, 1983.

Joyce, James. *A Portrait of the Artist as a Young Man.* 1916. Frogmore, Herts: Panther, 1977.

Orwell, George. *Nineteen Eighty-Four.* 1949. Harmondsworth: Penguin, 1954.

Stevenson, R. L. "The Strange Case of Dr Jekyll and Mr Hyde." In *The Strange Case of Dr Jekyll and Mr Hyde and Other Stories.* Ed. Jenni Calder. 1886. Harmondsworth: Penguin, 1979. 29–97.

SECONDARY SOURCES

IV. Studies of Diary Writing

Abbott, H. Porter. *Diary Fiction: Writing As Action.* Ithaca, New York: Cornell UP, 1984.

Barthes, Roland. "Deliberation." Trans. Richard Howard. In *A Barthes Reader.* Cape, 1982. 479–95.

Boerner, Peter. "The Significance of the Diary in Modern Literature." *Yearbook of General and Comparative Literature* 21 (1972): 41–45.

Bowring, Richard. "Japanese Diaries and the Nature of Literature." *Comparative Literature Studies* 18 (1981): 167–74.

Cardinal, Roger. "Unlocking the Diary." *Comparative Criticism* 12 (1990): 71–87.

Duyfhuizen, Bernard. "Diary Narratives in Fact and Fiction." *Novel* 19 (1985–86): 171–78. [A review article containing reviews of Abbott, Martens, and Mallon.]

Field, Trevor. *Form and Function in the Diary Novel.* Macmillan, 1989.

Fothergill, Robert. *Private Chronicles: A Study of English Diaries.* Oxford: Oxford UP, 1974.

Genette, Gérard. "Le Journal, l'antijournal." *Poétique* 47 (1981): 315–22. [A discussion of Barthes's "Délibération".]

Gristwood, Sarah. *Recording Angels: The Secret World of Women's Diaries.* Harrap, 1988.

Hassam, Andrew. "Style and Convention in the Diary: An Investigation with Reference to the Reader." Diss. U of Wales, 1983.

———. "Reading Other People's Diaries." *University of Toronto Quarterly* 56 (1987): 435–42.

———. "Literature, Culture and the Diary Novel." *Prose Studies* 13 (1990): 293–300.

Hogan, Rebecca. "Engendered Autobiographies: The Diary as a Feminine Form." *Prose Studies* 14 (1991): 95–107.

Kennedy, Alan. "Thinking the Thinking of Criticism." *University of Toronto Quarterly* 56 (1987): 443–51. [A review article containing a review of Abbott.]

Kuhn-Osius, K. Eckhard. "Making Loose Ends Meet: Private Journals in the Public Realm." *German Quarterly* 54 (1981): 166–76.

Mallon, Thomas. *A Book of One's Own: People and Their Diaries.* Picador, 1985.

Martens, Lorna. *The Diary Novel.* Cambridge: Cambridge UP, 1985.

Matthews, William. *British Diaries: An Annotated Bibliography of British Diaries Written between 1442 and 1942.* Cambridge: Cambridge UP, 1950.

————, and Robert Latham, eds. *The Diary of Samuel Pepys.* Vol. 1. Bell, 1970.

Miner, Earl. *Japanese Poetic Diaries.* Berkeley, CA: U of California P, 1969.

————. "Literary Diaries and the Boundaries of Literature." *Yearbook of General and Comparative Literature* 21 (1972): 46–52.

Nussbaum, Felicity. "Toward Conceptualizing Diary." In *Studies in Autobiography.* Ed. James Olney. Oxford UP, 1988. 128–40.

Ponsonby, Arthur. *English Diaries.* Methuen, 1923.

Prince, Gerald. "The Diary Novel: Notes for the Definition of a Sub-Genre." *Neophilologus* 59 (1975): 477–81.

Rainer, Tristine. *The New Diary: How to Use a Journal for Self-Guidance and Expanded Creativity.* Angus and Robertson, 1980.

Raoul, Valerie. *The French Fictional Journal: Fictional Narcissism / Narcissistic Fiction.* Toronto: U of Toronto P, 1980.

————. "Women and Diaries: Gender and Genre." *Mosaic* 22.3 (1989): 57–65.

Rousset, Jean. "Le Journal Intime, texte sans destinataire?" *Poétique* 56 (1983): 435–43.

Spalding, P. A. *Self-Harvest: A Study of Diaries and the Diarist.* Independent Press, 1949.

Willy, Margaret. *Three Women Diarists: Celia Fiennes, Dorothy Wordsworth, and Katherine Mansfield.* Writers and Their Work 173. British Council, 1964.

V. Studies of Autobiography

Eakin, Paul John. *Fictions in Autobiography: Studies in the Art of Self-Invention.* Princeton: Princeton UP, 1985.

————. "Philippe Lejeune and the Study of Autobiography." *Romance Studies* 8 (1986): 1–14.

Gratton, J. "*Roland Barthes par Roland Barthes:* Autobiography and the Notion of Expression." *Romance Studies* 8 (1986): 57–65.

Hassam, Andrew. "The Oscillating Text: A Reading of *The Private Papers of Henry Ryecroft.*" *English Literature in Transition* 28 (1985): 30–40.

————. "True Novel or Autobiography? The Case of B. S. Johnson's *Trawl*." *Prose Studies* 9 (1986): 62–72.

Kritzman, Lawrence D. "Autobiography: Readers and Texts." *Dispositio* 4 (1979): 117–21. [A review article containing a review of Lejeune's *Le Pacte Autobiographique*.]

Lejeune, Philippe. "Autobiography in the Third Person." Trans. Annette and Edward Tomarken. *New Literary History* 9 (1977): 27–50.

————. "The Autobiographical Contract." Trans. R. Carter. In *French Literary Theory Today*. Ed. Tzvetan Todorov. Cambridge: Cambridge UP, 1982. 192–222.

————. "Le Pacte Autobiographique (bis)." *Poétique* 56 (1983): 416–34.

————. "Making Ripples: A Reader's Chronicle." Trans. Michael Sheringham. *Romance Studies* 9 (1986): 21–34.

Loesberg, Jonathan. "Autobiography as Genre, Act of Consciousness, Text." *Prose Studies* 4 (1981): 169–85.

Mansell, Darrel. "Unsettling the Colonel's Hash: 'Fact' in Autobiography." *Modern Language Quarterly* 37 (1976): 115–32.

Olney, James, ed. *Autobiography: Essays Theoretical and Critical*. Princeton: Princeton UP, 1980.

————. *Studies in Autobiography*. Oxford UP, 1988.

Renza, Louis A. "The Veto of the Imagination: A Theory of Autobiography." *New Literary History* 9 (1977): 1–26. Rpt. in *Autobiography: Essays Theoretical and Critical*. Ed. James Olney. Princeton: Princeton UP, 1980. 268–95.

Ryan, Michael. "Self-Evidence." *Diacritics* 10.2 (1980): 2–16. [A review article of Lejeune's *Le Pacte Autobiographique*.]

Sturrock, John. "The New Model Autobiographer." *New Literary History* 9 (1977): 51–63.

VI.   Linguistics, Poetics, and Other Secondary Sources

Bacon, Francis. *Essays*. Dent, 1906.

Barthes, Roland. "The Discourse of History." In *The Rustle of Language*. Trans. Richard Howard. Oxford: Blackwell, 1986. 127–40.

Berger, Peter L., and Thomas Luckmann. *The Social Construction of Reality: A Treatise on the Sociology of Knowledge*. Allen Lane, 1967.

Borker, Ruth. "Anthropology: Social and Cultural Perspectives." *Women and Language in Literature and Society*. Ed. Sally McConnell-Ginet, Ruth Borker, and Nelly Furman. New York: Praeger, 1980. 26–44.

Bowie, Malcolm. "Jacques Lacan." In *Structuralism and Since: From Lévi-Strauss to Derrida*. Ed. John Sturrock. Oxford: Oxford UP, 1979. 116–53.

Bradbury, Malcolm, ed. *The Novel Today: Contemporary Writers on Modern Fiction*. Glasgow: Fontana/Collins, 1977.

————. "Modern Literary Theory: Its Place in Teaching." *Times Literary Supplement*. 6 Feb. 1981: 137.

Butor, Michel. "The Second Case: The Use of Personal Pronouns in the Novel." *New Left Review* 34 (Nov.–Dec. 1965): 61–8.

Carter, Paul. *The Road to Botany Bay: An Essay in Spatial History*. Faber, 1987.

Culler, Jonathan. *Structuralist Poetics*. Routledge, 1975.

Donovan, Josephine. "The Silence Is Broken." In *Women and Language in Literature and Society*. Ed. Sally McConnell-Ginet, Ruth Borker, and Nelly Furman. New York: Praeger, 1980. 205–18.

Eddins, Dwight. "John Fowles: Existence as Authorship." *Contemporary Literature* 17 (1976): 204–22.

Edwards, Gavin. "Narrative, Rites of Passage and the Early Modern Life-Cycle." *Trivium* 23 (1988): 115–26.

Fabb, Nigel and Alan Durant. "Ten Years On in the Linguistics of Writing." *Prose Studies* 10 (1987): 51–71.

Forster, E. M. *Aspects of the Novel*. 1927. Harmondsworth: Penguin, 1962.

Foucault, Michel. "What Is an Author?" In *Textual Strategies: Perspectives in Post-Structuralist Criticism*. Ed. Josué V. Harari. Methuen, 1980. 141–60.

Gallop, Jane. "The Mother Tongue." In *The Politics of Theory: Proceedings of the Essex Conference on the Sociology of Literature, July 1982*. Ed. Francis Barker et al. Colchester: U of Essex, 1983. 49–56.

————. "Snatches of Conversation." In *Women and Language in Literature and Society*. Ed. Sally McConnell-Ginet, Ruth Borker, and Nelly Furman. New York: Praeger, 1980. 274–83.

Genette, Gérard. *Narrative Discourse*. Trans. Jane E. Lewin. Oxford: Blackwell, 1980.

Gossman, Lionel. "History and Literature: Reproduction or Signification." In *The Writing of History: Literary Form and Historical Understanding*. Ed. Robert H. Canary and Henry Kozicki. Madison, Wisconsin: U of Wisconsin P, 1978. 3–39.

Haffenden, John. *Novelists in Interview*. Methuen, 1985.

Jacobus, Mary. "Is There a Woman in This Text?" *New Literary History* 14 (1982): 117–41.

Johnson, B. S. "Introduction." In *Aren't You Rather Young to be Writing Your Memoirs?* Hutchinson, 1973. 11–31.

Leech, Geoffrey. "Disjunctive Grammar in British Television Advertising." *Studia Neophilologica* 35 (1963): 256–64.

————. *English in Advertising*. Longman, 1966.

Lennox, Sara. "Trends in Literary Theory: The Female Aesthetic and German Women's Writing." *German Quarterly* 54 (1981): 63–75.

McEwan, Neil. *Perspective in British Historical Fiction Today*. Macmillan, 1987.

Mink, Louis O. "History and Fiction as Modes of Comprehension." *New Literary History* 1 (1970): 541–58.

————. "Narrative Form as a Cognitive Instrument." In *The Writing of History: Literary Form and Historical Understanding*. Ed. Robert H. Canary and Henry Kozicki. Madison, Wisconsin: U of Wisconsin P, 1978. 129–49.

Mistacco, Vicki. "The Theory and Practice of Reading Nouveaux Romans: Robbe-Grillet's *Topologie d'une cité fantôme*." In *The Reader in the Text: Essays on Audience and Interpretation*. Ed. Susan Suleiman and Inge Crosman. Princeton: Princeton UP, 1980. 371–400.

Norris, Christopher. *Deconstruction: Theory and Practice*. Methuen, 1982.

Roth, Paul A. "Narrative Explanations: The Case of History." *History and Theory* 27 (1988): 1–13.

Ruthven, K. K. *Feminist Literary Studies: An Introduction*. Cambridge: Cambridge UP, 1984.

Snyder, Joel, and Neil Walsh Allen. "Photography, Vision, and Representation." *Critical Inquiry* 2 (1975): 143–69.

Tosh, John. *The Pursuit of History: Aims, Methods, and New Directions in the Study of Modern History*. Longman, 1984.

Watson, Barbara Bellow. "Leaving the Safety of Myth: Doris Lessing's *The Golden Notebook* (1962)." In *Old Lines, New Forces: Essays of the Contemporary British Novel, 1960–1970*. Ed. Robert K. Morris. Cranbury, New Jersey: Fairleigh Dickinson UP, 1976. 12–37.

Watt, Ian. *The Rise of the Novel: Studies in Defoe, Richardson and Fielding*. 1957. Harmondsworth: Penguin, 1972.

Waugh, Patricia. *Metafiction: The Theory and Practice of Self-Conscious Fiction*. Methuen, 1984.

White, Hayden. "The Historical Text as Literary Artifact." In *The Writing of History: Literary Form and Historical Understanding*. Ed. Robert H. Canary and Henry Kozicki. Madison, Wisconsin: U of Wisconsin P, 1978. 41–62.

Wright, Elizabeth. "Modern Psychoanalytic Criticism." In *Modern Literary Theory: A Comparative Introduction*. Ed. Ann Jefferson and David Robey. Batsford Academic, 1982. 113–33.

————. *Psychoanalytic Criticism: Theory in Practice*. Methuen, 1984.

SUPPLEMENTARY BIBLIOGRAPHY

The following selected bibliography is intended to help readers who wish to pursue an interest in some of the lesser-known writers I discuss. Unless otherwise stated, the place of publication is London.

Eva Figes (b. 1932)

Novels

Equinox. Secker, 1966.
Winter Journey. Faber, 1967. New York: Hill & Wang, 1968.
Konek Landing. Faber, 1969.
B. Faber, 1972.
Days. Faber, 1974.
Nelly's Version. Secker, 1977. Hamish Hamilton, 1985.
Waking. Hamish Hamilton, 1981. New York: Pantheon, 1982.
Light. Hamish Hamilton, 1983. New York: Pantheon, 1983.
The Seven Ages. Hamish Hamilton, 1986.
Ghosts. Hamish Hamilton, 1988.
The Tree of Knowledge. Sinclair-Stevenson, 1990.

Secondary Material

Conradi, Peter. "Eva Figes." In *British Novelists Since 1960*. Ed. Jay L.
        Halio. Detroit: Gale, 1983. Vol. 14 of *Dictionary of Literary Biogra-
        phy*. 298–302.
Figes, Eva. Interview. *The Imagination on Trial*. Ed. Alan Burns and
        Charles Sugnet. Allison & Busby, 1981. 31–39.
Friedman, Ellen G. "'Utterly Other Discourse': The Anticanon of Experi-
        mental Women Writers from Dorothy Richardson to Christine
        Brooke-Rose." *Modern Fiction Studies* 34 (1988): 353–370.
McLaughlin, Brian Gerard. "Structures of Identity: A Reading of the Self-
        Provoking Fiction of Christine Brooke-Rose, Bryan Stanley
        Johnson, Eva Figes and Paul West." *Dissertation Abstracts Inter-
        national* 42 (1982): 4460(A). Pennsylvania State U.

Margaret Forster (b. 1938)

Novels

Dames' Delight. Cape, 1964.
The Bogeyman. Secker, 1965. New York: Putnam, 1966.
Georgy Girl. Secker, 1965. New York: Berkley, 1966.
The Travels of Maudie Tipstaff. Secker, 1967. New York: Stein & Day,
        1967.
The Park. Secker, 1968.
Miss Owen-Owen Is at Home. Secker, 1969. Rpt. as *Miss Owen-Owen*.
        New York: Simon, 1969.
Fenella Phizackerley. Secker, 1970; New York: Simon, 1971.
Mr Bone's Retreat. Secker, 1971; New York: Simon, 1971.
The Seduction of Mrs Pendlebury. Secker, 1974.

William Makepeace Thackeray, Memoirs of a Victorian Gentleman.
    Secker, 1979.
Mother Can You Hear Me? Secker, 1980.
The Bride of Lowther Fell: A Romance. Secker, 1980. New York: Athe-
    neum, 1981.
Marital Rites. Secker, 1981. New York: Atheneum, 1982.
Private Papers. Chatto, 1986.
Have the Men Had Enough? Chatto, 1989.
Lady's Maid. Chatto, 1990.
Battle for Christabel. Chatto, 1991.

Rayner Heppenstall (1911–81)

Novels

The Blaze of Noon. Secker, 1939. Allison & Busby, 1980.
Saturnine. Secker, 1943.
The Lesser Infortune. Cape, 1953.
The Greater Infortune [revision of *Saturnine*]. Peter Owen, 1960.
The Woodshed. Barrie & Rockliff, 1962.
The Connecting Door. Barrie & Rockliff, 1962.
The Shearers. Hamish Hamilton, 1969.
Two Moons. Allison & Busby, 1977.
The Pier. Allison & Busby, 1986.

Secondary Material

Heppenstall, Rayner. *The Master Eccentric: The Journals of Rayner
    Heppenstall 1969–81.* Ed. Jonathan Goodman. Allison & Busby,
    1986.
Higdon, David Leon. *Shadows of the Past in Contemporary British
    Fiction.* Macmillan, 1984.
Monod, Sylvère. "Rayner Heppenstall and the *Nouveau Roman.*"
    Imagined Worlds. Methuen, 1968.

B. S. Johnson (1933–73)

Novels

Travelling People. Constable, 1963.
Albert Angelo. Constable, 1964.
Trawl. Secker, 1966.
The Unfortunates. Panther, 1969.
House Mother Normal. Collins, 1971.
Christie Malry's Own Double-Entry. Collins, 1973. New York: Viking,
    1973.

See the Old Lady Decently. Hutchinson, 1975. New York: Viking, 1975.

Poetry

Poems. Constable, 1964. New York: Chilmark, 1964.
Poems Two. Trigram, 1972.

Short Story Collections

Statements Against Corpses [with Zulfikar Ghose]. Constable, 1964.
Aren't You Rather Young to Be Writing Your Memoirs? Hutchinson, 1973.

Secondary Material

Curtis, Tony. "The Poetry of B. S. Johnson." *Anglo-Welsh Review* 26 (Autumn 1976): 130–42.

Hassam, Andrew. "True Novel or Autobiography? The Case of B. S. Johnson's *Trawl.*" *Prose Studies* 9 (1986): 62–72.

Levitt, Morton P. "The Novels of B. S. Johnson: Against the War against Joyce." *Modern Fiction Studies* 27 (1981–82): 571–86.

———. "B. S. Johnson." In *British Novelists Since 1960.* Ed. Jay L. Halio. Detroit: Gale, 1983. Vol. 14 of *Dictionary of Literary Biography.* 438–44.

Lilly, Mark. "The Novels of B. S. Johnson." *Planet* 26/27 (Winter 1974/75): 33–40.

McLaughlin, Brian Gerard. "Structures of Identity: A Reading of the Self-Provoking Fiction of Christine Brooke-Rose, Bryan Stanley Johnson, Eva Figes and Paul West." *Dissertation Abstracts International* 42 (1982): 4460(A). Pennsylvania State U.

Ommundsen, Wenche. "Self-Conscious Fiction and Literary Theory: David Lodge, B. S. Johnson, and John Fowles." *Dissertation Abstracts International* 47 (1986): 2170(A). U of Melbourne.

Pacey, Philip. "Merely Human—The Writings of B. S. Johnson." *Stand* 13. 2 (1972): 61–64.

———. "I on Behalf of Us: B. S. Johnson 1933–1973." *Stand* 15. 2 (1974): 19–26.

———. "B. S. Johnson and Wales." *Anglo-Welsh Review* 63 (1978): 73–80.

Parrinder, Patrick. "Pilgrim's Progress: The Novels of B. S. Johnson." *Critical Quarterly,* 19.2 (1977): 45–59.

Review of Contemporary Fiction 5 (1984). B. S. Johnson/Jean Rhys Number.

Ryf, Robert S. "Character and Imagination in the Experimental Novel." *Modern Fiction Studies* 20 (1974): 317–27.

————. "B. S. Johnson and the Frontiers of Fiction." *Critique: Studies in Modern Fiction* 19.1 (1977): 58–74.

Tredell, Nicolas. "See B.S. Johnson Decently." *PN Review* 14.1 (1987): 47–52; 14.2 (1987): 58–62.

Robert Nye (b. 1939)

Novels

Doubtfire. Calder & Boyars, 1967. New York: Hill & Wang, 1968.

Falstaff. Hamish Hamilton, 1976. Boston: Little, 1976.

Merlin. Hamish Hamilton, 1978. New York: Putnam, 1979.

Faust. Hamish Hamilton, 1980. New York: Putnam, 1981.

The Voyage of the Destiny. Hamish Hamilton, 1982. New York: Putnam, 1982.

The Facts of Life. Hamish Hamilton, 1983.

The Memoirs of Lord Byron. Hamish Hamilton, 1989.

The Life and Death of My Lord Gilles de Rais. Hamish Hamilton. 1990.

Short Story Collections

Tales I Told my Mother. Calder & Boyars, 1969. New York: Hill & Wang, 1970.

Facts of Life and Other Fictions. Hamish Hamilton, 1983.

Secondary Material

Allen, Elizabeth. "Robert Nye." In *British Novelists Since 1960.* Ed. Jay L. Halio. Detroit: Gale, 1983. Vol. 14 of *Dictionary of Literary Biography.* 564-71.

McEwan, Neil. *Perspective in British Historical Fiction Today.* Macmillan, 1987.

Ann Quin (1936–73)

Novels

Berg. John Calder, 1964. Quartet, 1977. Paladin, 1989. New York: Scribner, 1965.

Three. Calder & Boyars, 1966; New York: Scribner, 1966.

Passages. Calder & Boyars, 1969.

Tripticks. Calder & Boyars, 1972.

"From *The Unmapped Country,* an Unfinished Novel." In *Beyond the Words: Eleven Writers in Search of a New Fiction.* Ed. Giles Gordon. Hutchinson, 1975. 250–74.

Short Stories

"Every Cripple Has His Own Way of Walking." *Nova* 1966 (Dec.): 125–35.
"Living in the Present" [with Robert Sward]. *Ambit* 34 (1968): 20–21.
"Tripticks." *Ambit* 35 (1968): 9–16.
"Never Trust a Man Who Bathes with His Fingernails." *El Corno Emplumado* (Mexico City) 1968.
"Motherlogue." *Transatlantic Review* 32 (Summer 1969): 101–5. Rpt. in *Anti-Story: An Anthology of Experimental Fiction*. Ed. Philip Stevick. New York: Free Press, 1971.
"Eyes That Watch Behind the Wind." *Signature Anthology*. Calder & Boyars, 1975. 131–49.

Secondary Material

Barber, Dulan. "Afterword to *Berg*." *Berg*. Quartet, 1977. 169–77.
Boyars, Marion. "Note on Ann Quin." In *Beyond the Words: Eleven Writers in Search of a New Fiction*. Ed. Giles Gordon. Hutchinson, 1975. 251.
Dunn, Nell. *Talking to Women*. 1965. Pan, 1966. 108–29.
Kitchen, Paddy. "Catherine Wheel: Recollections of Ann Quin." *London Magazine* 19 (June 1979): 50–57.
Mackrell, Judith. "Ann Quin." In *British Novelists Since 1960*. Ed. Jay L. Halio. Detroit: Gale, 1983. Vol. 14 of *Dictionary of Literary Biography*. 608–14.
Quin, Ann. "Leaving School." *London Magazine* July 1966: 63–68.
Sewell, Brocard. *Like Black Swans: Some People and Themes*. Padstow, Cornwall: Tabb House, 1982. 183–92.
Stevick, Philip. "Voices in the Head: Style and Consciousness in the Fiction of Ann Quin." *Breaking the Sequence: Women's Experimental Fiction*. Ed. Ellen G. Friedman and Miriam Fuchs. Princeton, NJ: Princeton UP, 1989. 231–39.
White, John. J. *Mythology in the Modern Novel: A Study of Prefigurative Techniques*. Princeton, NJ: Princeton UP, 1971. 186–87.
Wilmott, R. D. *A Bibliography of Works by and about Ann Quin*. Ealing Miscellany, No. 23. Ealing College of Higher Education, School of Library and Information Studies, 1982.

Jane Rogers (b. 1952)

Novels

Separate Tracks. Faber, 1983.
Her Living Image. Faber, 1984
The Ice Is Singing. Faber, 1987.
Mr Wroe's Virgins. Faber, 1991.

Emma Tennant (b. 1937)

Novels

The Colour of Rain. [As Catherine Aydy.] Weidenfeld, 1964; Faber, 1988.

The Time of the Crack. Cape, 1973. Rpt. as *The Crack.* Faber, 1985.

The Last of the Country House Murders. Cape, 1974. New York: Nelson, 1976.

Hotel de Dream. Gollancz, 1976.

The Bad Sister. Gollancz, 1978. New York: Coward McCann, 1978.

Wild Nights. Cape, 1979. New York: Harcourt, 1980.

Alice Fell. Cape, 1980.

Queen of Stones. Cape, 1982.

Woman Beware Woman. Cape, 1983. Rpt. as *The Half-Mother.* Boston: Little, 1985.

Black Marina. Faber, 1985.

The Adventures of Robina, by Herself. Faber, 1986.

The House of Hospitalities. Viking, 1987.

A Wedding of Cousins. Viking, 1988.

The Magic Drum. Viking, 1989.

Two Women of London: The Strange Case of Ms Jekyll and Mrs Hyde. Faber, 1989.

Sisters and Strangers. Grafton, 1990.

Secondary Material

Alexander, Flora. *Contemporary Women Novelists.* Edward Arnold, 1989.

Lambert, Georgina L. "Emma Tennant." In *British Novelists Since 1960.* Ed. Jay L. Halio. Detroit: Gale, 1983. Vol. 14 of *Dictionary of Literary Biography.* 708–15.

Index

About the Author

ANDREW HASSAM is a lecturer in English at Trinity College, Carmarthen, Wales. He currently holds a visiting research fellowship at the National Library in Canberra, Australia. He has published scholarly articles in journals in Britain, Canada, Australia, and the United States, as well as short stories in literary magazines. He is presently at work on a reference companion to an international representation of diary fiction.